HOW TO BE A complete and utter failure in life, work and everything

P9-CSU-636

Prentice Hall LIFE

If life is what you make it, then making it better starts here.

What we learn today can change our lives tomorrow. It can change our goals or change our minds; open up new opportunities or simply inspire us to make a difference. That's why we have created a new breed of books that do more to help you make more of *your* life.

Whether you want more confidence or less stress, a new skill or a different perspective, we've designed *Prentice Hall Life* books to help you to make a change for the better. Together with our authors we share a commitment to bring you the brightest ideas and best ways to manage your life, work and wealth.

In these pages we hope you'll find the ideas you need for the life *you* want. Go on, help yourself.

It's what you make it

* * *

HOW TO BE A complete

and utter

failure

in life, work and

everything

44$\frac{1}{2}$ steps to lasting underachievement

Second edition

STEVE McDERMOTT

Harlow, England • London • New York • Boston • San Francisco • Toronto • Sydney • Singapore • Hong Kong
Tokyo • Seoul • Taipei • New Delhi • Cape Town • Madrid • Mexico City • Amsterdam • Munich • Paris • Milan

PEARSON EDUCATION LIMITED

Edinburgh Gate
Harlow CM20 2JE
Tel: +44 (0)1279 623623
Fax: +44 (0)1279 431059
Website: www.pearsoned.co.uk

First published 2002
Second edition published in Great Britain in 2007

© Steve McDermott 2002
© Pearson Education Limited 2007

The right of Steve McDermott to be identified as author of this work has been asserted
by him in accordance with the Copyright, Designs and Patents Act 1988.

ISBN: 978-0-273-70607-6

British Library Cataloguing-in-Publication Data
A catalogue record for this book is available from the British Library

10 9 8 7 6 5 4 3 2 1
11 10 09 08 07

Designed by Claire Brodmann Book Designs, Lichfield, Staffs.
Typeset by 30
Printed and bound in Great Britain by Ashford Colour Press, Gosport

The publishers' policy is to use paper manufactured from sustainable forests.

THIS BOOK IS dedicated to

my inspiration, and the

true source of

my success,

my beautiful wife

Candy and our

fantastic children,

Tom, Finlay and

Megan.

Preface to the second edition

'I went to a bookstore,' says the great deadpan American comedian Steven Wright, *'and I asked the saleswoman, "Where's the self-help section?" She said if she told me it would defeat the purpose.'*

Welcome to the second edition of this unique, and best-selling, self-unimprovement guide™. Packed with all the stuff from first time around plus five brand new steps, loads more stories, examples, jokes, actions not to take and exercises not to do. So now you can also learn how to be a complete and utter failure at first impressions, leadership, communication, teamwork and customer service.

After the first edition of this guide was published, many people from all around the world got in touch via email (**steve@stevemcdermott.com**) to say that they had ignored my advice to not do the exact opposite of what I had written. Of all the cheek. (In Indonesia the book title translates as 'Look who's the loser here' which I think is brilliant.)

Many people wanted to share with me how the guide had inspired them to take action and change something. Some changed their jobs, some changed their business, some changed their minds and some even changed their partners.

Now some authors may promise to change your life in seven days, which is of course complete rubbish. They can't change anything. However, you can. So please, this time, don't go doing the exact opposite of what I say otherwise I'll be deluged with loads more success stories and nobody wants that, do they?

How to get the most from this guide

DON'T READ IT. JUST LEAVE IT by the side of the bed gathering dust. It can then act as a powerful reminder that the worst thing you can possibly do, in order to sabotage your chances of future failure, is open up your mind to any new ideas or take any sort of action.

Quotes to avoid

'I was going to buy a copy of "The Power of Positive Thinking" and then thought what the hell good would that do?' **Anon**

It might be annoying but you can't beat a good quote to get you fired up. Or just to make you laugh. That's why I've put together this handy reference of inspirational, profound and sometimes funny ideas, from some of the best thinkers that have ever lived. By carefully steering clear of these, and similar sources of wit and wisdom, you should be able to remain totally unmotivated and miserable.

Action not to take

Is knowledge power? No. It's what you do with what you know that counts. It's a bit like if you can read but never bother to read a book, then you are really as ignorant as someone who can't read. That's why you mustn't do any of the simple, practical exercises in these sections throughout the guide. I've only put them here so you know what to avoid. It would ruin your chances of lasting underachievement if you accidentally performed just one. Don't, even for one moment, consider doing any of them.

Interactivity

Longest word – There aren't many big words in this guide, but if you want to stop yourself going to sleep, why not see if you can spot the longest. Personally, I wouldn't bother. The answer is at the back – simply look there now if you want to cheat.

Most obscure reference – Nearly all the ideas in this guide could be understood by a child of four, so hopefully you've got one to explain things to you. However, there may be a few obscure references, mostly from my personal life, you don't get. My editor said to remove any anecdotes that wouldn't travel, whatever that means, but I haven't really bothered. However, there is one particular esoteric reference that is peculiar to my part of the world and a certain era in time. I wonder if you can spot what it is. For the workshy, the answer is also at the back.

Diagrams

All books about business, careers and personal development have diagrams. So we thought we'd better stuff a few in too.

Here is one to get you started:

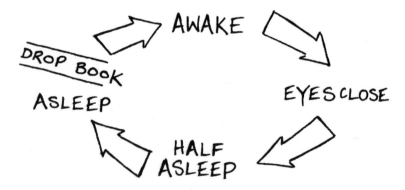

FIG 1 The effect an increasing number of circle flow charts have on the reader

Political correctness

Throughout this guide when the pronoun 'he' is used, as it is in the sentence 'He is an utter failure in life, work and everything', I simply mean a human being. Obviously I also mean 'she'. And when I use 'she' I also, of course, mean 'he'. If I say 'he or she' I also mean both sexes. If I don't say 'he or she', don't take this to mean I don't mean either sex. Hope that's cleared up the awkwardness of this. Will someone please hurry up and invent a word that means both.[1]

Thinking style

As Scott Fitzgerald said: 'The test of a first-rate intelligence is the ability to hold two opposed ideas in the mind at the same time, and still retain the ability to function. Without steam coming out of your ears.' I added that last bit. One of the keys to success is to open-mindedly consider new – what might sometimes seem bizarre – ideas, even if they may conflict with your long-standing beliefs and convictions. However, don't be seduced by this way of thinking – you mustn't stop immediately dismissing things out of hand.

Don't stop letting any factual inaccuracies in this guide drive you to distraction either. For instance, another way of expressing Scott Fitzgerald's point of view would be to adopt the thinking style of Janus, the two-faced Greek god. He of course had the advantage of not only literally testing whether two heads are in fact better than one, but was also capable of having two different thoughts at the same time. You may say to me, 'Hang on a minute, Steve, wasn't Janus a two-headed Roman god?' You may be right. Please feel free to waste more of your valuable time and energy finding out what's wrong with this guide rather than finding what's right. Just don't write to tell me the full nit-picking details. OK?

[1] Since the first edition someone has. A reader Jethro Adlington wrote and suggested the term Heshe (pronounced 'Hesh') so you would say, 'Heshe was a complete failure.'

Author's warning

Remember I'm strongly suggesting that you don't think about the direct opposite of the steps in this guide, especially right now just before you read it, as this could seriously damage your chances of becoming a complete and utter failure in life, work and everything.

Introduction

Often the hardest thing to change is how you think. I'm from the county of Yorkshire, England. So is my wife's Uncle Richard. Now in case you don't know, folk from Yorkshire are known for their down-to-earth, no-nonsense approach to life (others would call us opinionated but they'd be wrong).

Anyway, I'm in the local pub – The Gaping Goose – with Uncle Richard and he's telling me that his wife, Aunty Anne-Marie, is having a minor eye operation. It's the one where they use a laser to correct your vision, and the surgeon has said she should be able to see, without the aid of spectacles, within 24 hours. Uncle Richard is finding this hard to believe.

I tell Uncle Richard, 'I know why that is.' You see, coincidentally, only the day before I attended a conference where one of the speakers was an American lady who was a world-renowned expert on alternative health treatments. She talked about how she had cured herself of a tumour the size of a basketball growing in her abdomen in, get this, just six weeks. She explained that through cell regeneration all of us get an entirely new body over a period of time, and that different parts of us regenerate at different speeds.

For instance, she pointed out that if you've ever had a suntan, you'll know it takes about two weeks to fade. That's because it takes the cells in your skin about two weeks to replace themselves totally with new cells. She then went on to say that your liver takes about three months, your stomach lining three weeks and your eyeball about 24 to 48 hours. So, although when you poke it it feels hard, in fact it's a whole new eyeball.

In case you're interested, she went on to say how come, then, we get disease; how come if we have a diseased liver our body doesn't just replace it with a healthy one? The answer, she said, is that each cell in your body carries a programme or a memory. Somehow disease causes this programme to be altered, and so instead of regenerating healthy tissue and organs, we now continue to replicate unhealthy ones. To cure herself of her tumour in such a short space of time, she believed that somehow she had developed the ability to interrupt the programme and reprogramme her cells back to the healthy memory.

Now when I told Uncle Richard all of this, do you know what he said? He said, 'B******s'. (This is a popular Yorkshire swear word that refers to a part of the male anatomy.)

Now I don't want you to think that you need to have any more of an open mind than Uncle Richard to get the most out of this guide. Don't stop thinking what you've always thought – that way you'll only learn what you already know. Or as someone once said: 'Faced with the choice between changing one's mind and proving that there is no need to do so, almost everybody gets busy on the proof.'

B**×@+*@S

This guide originally began life with me pondering some profound questions like: 'What is the secret to becoming an outstanding failure?' 'Can anyone become a failure?' 'Having become a failure, how do you remain so, year after miserable year?' and 'Why does sour cream have a sell-by date?' You'll find the answers to all these questions, apart from the last one, in these pages.

Having studied individuals, from all walks of life, who have massively underachieved, I've come to the startling conclusion that all these very different people share the exact same strategies for failure. It's these strategies they use each and every day in order to become absolute wasters and washouts.

True failure, however, comes at a price. Did you know that it can take a lot more work and energy to become a complete and utter useless loser in life, work and everything, than it can to become an outstanding success? That's because amongst other things, as we'll discover later, successful people don't ever feel like they work for a living, whereas most failures dislike or even hate their jobs and sweat blood and tears to get nowhere fast or, if they are really good, even to go backwards.

What did I learn when I examined some of our best, most natural failures? Well, just look at most of your relatives, friends and colleagues. For this select band, failure is as easy as breathing. To them it's as easy to fail as it is to put the alarm clock on snooze for just a few more minutes. And of course the truth is that, for most of us, failure is an unconscious process. We fail without having to think about it. Over the next few minutes,[1] I will clearly show you what outstanding failures think, say and consistently do, or most of the time don't do, to screw up their chances of success.

Of course, for the sake of balance, for many years I've studied successful organizations and individuals too. I figure if we know their specific strategies for success, and then do the exact opposite, this will get us way beyond the level of mediocre failure. Although, I know most of you would be delighted to settle for that.

In this guide at last I will reveal the secret, yet simple, $44^{1}/_{2}$ tried, tested and proven steps that, should you follow them, are guaranteed to propel you into the slow lane of total inadequacy.

I wish you every success on your journey to becoming a total failure.

---

[1] It should take a bit longer than a few minutes to read this guide but hey, I know you've probably got the attention span of a goldfish. That's why I wouldn't suggest you must read every word, *twice*, rather than just flicking through, to gain maximum value.

PS The good news is that you may already have a head start in the failure race. In a survey, 10% of people in the UK thought they would be better off dead, 25% could see no hope for the future and 33% described themselves as downright miserable most of the time. If you are already part of this 68% majority, well done, your failure is already assured.

Step one Don't decide what you want. If you do decide what you want, don't think about why you want it. And if you do decide why you want it, commit to believing you can't have it.

Quote to avoid

'If we don't change our direction, we are likely to end up where we are going.'

Chinese proverb

Let's start at the beginning. The worst thing you can do, if you are truly committed to being one of life's failures, is to think clearly about what success means to you. We know that the best failures manage to avoid, at all costs, contemplating this most emotive of words.

On the other hand, it has been proven beyond any doubt, in study after study, that so-called high achievers have clearly defined what they want to do with their lives. And have lots and lots of reasons why they want to do it. They have a crystal-clear vision of the future. They know what they love to do. And have set goals that will enable them to do what they love to do. Goals that allow them to chase their passion, not their pension. Most importantly, these people also have a set of empowering beliefs that support them in creating the life they want to lead.

Yet the fact remains that very few people give the question of success, and what it means, any serious consideration. It shouldn't be surprising that so few achieve success, because so few know what it actually is. Winston Churchill thought success was 'the ability to go from one failure to another with no loss of enthusiasm'. Another man, called Earl Nightingale, can you believe spent 25 years thinking about success before coming up with what he claimed was the following definitive definition: 'Success is the progressive realization of a worthy ideal or goal.'

Let's see if we can take some of these words and figure out what the heck Earl was talking about.

1. Progressive

Success is not something that happens now and again. It builds up over time. Earl thought that success was a journey, not a destination. He said the fun was as much in the travelling as it was in the arriving, or as Louis L'Amour says: 'The trail is the thing, not the end of the trail. Travel too fast and you miss all you are travelling for.' Also, the distance a person goes is not as important as the direction. Or as a friend of mine, Glen McCoy, would put it: 'Success to me is taking action, however small the step, in a direction that builds.' Crucially, whether or not you arrive at your destination is not half as important as the type of person you become as you travel.

2. Realization

Means the more you think about and focus on success on the inside, the more it materializes on the outside. Or in other words, if you can hold it in your head, you can hold it in your hand. Everything that exists was created twice – even you, some would say. If you are sitting down as you read this, the solid chair you are sitting on right now once existed only as a thought inside someone's head. Then it was turned into a blueprint and finally into a real chair. But it all starts with a thought, and over time thoughts become things. Earl simply believed that if you controlled your thoughts, you controlled your life.

3. Worthy ideal or goal

Earl said this stood for an idea that you had fallen in love with. A goal that consumes your emotional, intellectual and physical self. He felt you should ask not, is this a worthy goal, but is the goal worthy of me? Is it worthy of my attention? Is it something I should be trading the days of my life for?

DON'T STOP putting off making the most important decision you could ever make.

Of course, we should take the Uncle Richard stance on this and believe Earl was talking complete rubbish, but on the off-chance that after 25 years of study he just might be right, this means you can easily apply the same formula to failure. Failure must be progressive too. It's also a journey. Focus on failure on the inside and you can manifest it on the outside. Instead of a worthy goal, have an unworthy goal like, say, just to own material or superficial things – cars, houses, boats, money and the like. As we'll discover in more depth later, this is the perfect strategy for never-ending failure.

Here is a second, much shorter definition of success: it's a decision. And the decision is: what do you want to be, do and have? Just like the man who got off a boat in America at the beginning of the last century. He was a poor immigrant with just one dollar in his pocket. Over the next 20 years he went on to found one of the most successful chains of restaurants in the country. When asked when he had realized he was a success, he replied it was when he first got off the boat and decided to open a chain of restaurants. In that moment of decision he became already successful.

In some 15 years of working with hundreds of individuals, I know only a tiny percentage of the population have made that decision. The vast majority, which probably includes you, are helping the small few live the life of their dreams. Because you see, if you don't think about the future, you don't have one. So don't do it. Don't stop putting off making the most important decision you could ever make.

Besides, even if you were to think about what you want to be, do and have, why take the risk of being disappointed? As children, all of us dream about what we could achieve. My advice is, don't think about what your dream was. Don't think about what your dream is right at this moment. Don't imagine that it's still possible to live it. Don't stop being realistic or lowering your sights. Don't be an ambitious dreamer. Don't pay any mind to Walt Disney who said, 'If you can dream it, you can do it.' Come off it Walt, I suppose next you'll be saying we all have the opportunity to pursue our heart's desire. Most people wait until they've been made redundant or fired before they feel they have the freedom to pursue their dreams passionately. So should you. This is perhaps the best way of wasting years of your life.

The good news for students of failure is that, even if you do decide what you really want, you'll probably never take action to make it happen. For example, in a survey which asked people who had reached the ripe old age of 100 what they most regretted, they said they wished they had taken more risks and done the things that made them feel happy. If you want to be able to say the same thing when you are 100 years of age, commit right now to drifting aimlessly through your life. Of course, being a highly trained pessimist, you won't make it that far because you'll die younger. But trust me, it will have seemed like 100 years.

Action not to take

We'll go into this in more detail throughout the rest of the guide, but for now don't ever take the time, on a regular basis, to define what success means to you. Don't take a few minutes to write down what success would look, feel and sound like for you right now in your life and in, say, five years' time.

Don't think about what's most important to you and what you most enjoy doing. Don't contemplate what makes you most happy, what you enjoy most and which people you'd like to spend most of your time with. Don't ask people you care about what success means to them. We do know that the more time you spend thinking about it, the more likely it is that it will come true. So be very careful.

Don't consider, from this moment onwards, the direction you'd like your life to take. Don't develop a magnificent obsession. Don't let the words of comedian Danny Kaye inspire you: 'Life is a great big canvas, and you should throw all the paint on it you can.' By the way, to have something different in your life, whether it's a new house or relationship, you are by definition going to have to do something different and become someone different to the person you are today. Otherwise, you'd have those things right now.

Unfortunately, if you do think about these things it will create anything from slight dissatisfaction to even unbearable pain about your current circumstances. And we know that dissatisfaction and pain are the fastest ways to get you to pull your finger out, change and do something about it. And we wouldn't want that, would we?

Step two

Don't do things on purpose.

Quote to avoid

Some luck lies in not getting what you thought you wanted but getting what you have, which once you have it, you may be smart enough to see is what you would have wanted had you known. **Garrison Keillor**

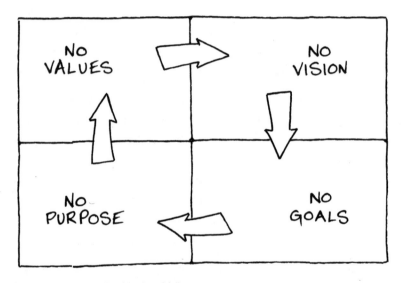

FIG 2 The four building blocks of failure

This is what the eminent psychiatrist Dr Anthony Clare had to say about happiness in an interview I once read: 'It's not simply a matter of having friends, but of feeling a part of something bigger than oneself: whether through family, work or community. That's why World War Two veterans often say that, despite the hardships, the war was one of the happiest times of their lives. War gave them "a sense of comradeship", a "common purpose" and a feeling of doing something worthwhile.' Or put another way by William Cowper: 'The only true happiness comes from squandering ourselves for a purpose.'

Most of us have no sense of purpose whatsoever. And we are unlikely to find one if we never think of looking. So what is purpose? In a business sense it would be: 'What are you in business to do? Why does your business exist?' Not surprisingly, the very worst performing businesses can never accurately answer this question.

In a personal sense it would be: 'Why were you put on the planet? Why are you here? What is it your mission to fulfil?' Remember in the excellent animated film *Toy Story 2*, Woody, the cowboy doll, has to decide what is his purpose. Is it to be a collector's piece and spend all his time in a museum, behind glass, protected forever from human touch? Or is it to be a real toy, played with by children, even though he knows one day this means he will be placed on the top shelf all battered and broken? Woody decides on his true purpose. (If you haven't seen the film I won't spoil it for you by telling you what he decides – even though someone did spoil the film *Sixth Sense* for me by pointing out, long before I saw it, that the character Bruce Willis plays is in fact a ghost. Whoops, you did know that, didn't you?)

You mustn't become as clear as Woody about your own purpose. Because if I've noticed one thing above any other that can aid your attempts at failure, it's having a complete lack of purpose. Many have a nagging thought that goes something like: 'What if I get to the end of my life and find that I have just lived the length of it? I want to have lived the width of it as well.'

Have you heard about the Buddhist monk who walked up to a hot dog vendor and said, 'Make me one with everything'? If only it was as easy as that. So how do you know when you're lacking meaning to your life? Well, often it's when you've attained all the material things, like houses and flashy cars, but you still feel empty on the inside or, as Andy Warhol observed: 'I am a deeply superficial person.' This is very reassuring because, as you look at all those people you envy for their outward material success, you can now take some perverse satisfaction from the fact that some are feeling, on the inside, just as miserable as you are. It would appear ours is a world where people don't know what they want and are willing to go through hell to get it.

Now unlike goals, purpose isn't something you set. The trouble with purpose is it's something you were born with. It's already inside you just waiting to be discovered. Which is why you must be careful you don't trip over yours by accident. Here is how Mary Dunbar puts it: 'We are each gifted in a unique and important way. It is our privilege and adventure to discover our own special light.' Or as Victor Frankl, author of *Man's Search for Meaning*, says: 'Everyone has their own specific vocation or mission in life to carry out. A concrete assignment which demands fulfilment. Therein they cannot be replaced, nor can their life be repeated. Thus, everyone's task is as unique as is their opportunity to implement it.'

THE TROUBLE with
purpose is it's something
you were born with.
It's **already** inside you
just **waiting** to be
discovered.

So how do you ensure you don't discover your purpose? Here are a few quick tips.

Don't stop thinking that your job and your purpose are the same

Successful people know that they could have up to four or five different careers, never mind jobs. They ensure their purpose aligns with their work but it isn't their work. Failures let their job define who they are. Which means if they change, or worse still lose their job, their self-esteem suffers.

Don't stop thinking that your purpose is your relationships

Not only do failures let their job define who they are but they let the same thing happen with relationships. Now have you noticed relationships change? If you are defined by your role of husband or wife, what happens if you get divorced or your partner dies?

Don't align your goals to your purpose

Have you been so busy climbing the ladder of success that you never notice whether it's leaning against the right wall? If you have lots of goals but don't align them to a clear sense of purpose, you will never feel you are creating anything lasting or worthwhile.

Don't stop thinking that your purpose must be outwardly impressive

My wife Candy, as a former nurse, gets concerned that some people I talk to about personal development may think it's all about making loads of money, being a striving big shot, a captain of industry, an entrepreneur and the like. She reminds me to tell people that if you positively change the life of just one person you can count yourself a success. (By the way, if success ever feels like you're striving rather than stretching, then you are definitely not doing things on purpose.)

Don't stop thinking that your purpose means you must be a martyr

If you think you've discovered your purpose but you still loathe what you do, if it feels hard and includes the maximum amount of pain and suffering, then you are deluding yourself. However, if you find something you love to do, then you'll never work another day in your life. Your purpose should fit you like a glove, not be determined by what others think you should be and do. At work, home or play, you'll feel your purpose permeates everything you do. Knowing your purpose brings a profound sense of peace, which is something that most people wouldn't usually associate with success. Whereas not knowing your purpose explains why you suffer from those unsettling feelings from time to time, leading to thinking about resigning from your job, but never quite working up the nerve to do so.

Don't stop thinking that your purpose must sound complex, be difficult to write down and remember

Have you seen those company purpose or mission statements, in their gold frames, that no one can remember a single word of, including customers? Well, if you follow that format your purpose won't be memorable, inspire you or make you leap out of bed every morning. So don't, whatever you do, aim to end up with a simple but powerful statement about why you are here and what you are here to do. Don't create a set of words that causes you to feel deeply what your life is about. That when you read them your emotions, and a voice inside your head, tell you: 'Yes, now I think about it, this is what I've always done and enjoy doing and can always see myself doing.'

Action not to take

Don't think about these four questions from Robert Allen, author of *The Road To Wealth*:

1. What are the seven things I absolutely love to do?
2. What are the seven things I am good at, have a talent for, or other people tell me I'm good at?
3. What is it absolutely essential for me to do in life?
4. What do I feel I ought or would like to be doing?

And don't think about the legacy you want to leave. Don't think about what you would want a letter to your grandchildren to say about the life you've led. Don't think about leaving your song unsung. Totally ignore the advice of the painter Ashley Jackson: 'Years go by fast as Catseyes on a motorway. The art of living is to make use of what you've got and use it to the full. Most people do not know what they are living for. But once you have found out, you have the jewel of life.' Comedian Demetri Martin puts it another way: 'I ordered a wake-up call the other day. The phone rang and a woman's voice said, "What the hell are you doing with your life?"'

Step three
Don't stop working for a living.

Quote to avoid

' Work is more fun than fun. ' Noël Coward

Do you work for a living? Do you unenthusiastically drag yourself out of bed every morning for another boring day, doing a job which at the best you don't really care about and at the worst you loathe? You do? Excellent, you're well on the way to a totally unfulfilled life. At least you can console yourself with this common excuse: 'One day when I've got enough money, when the kids have grown up, when . . . . (fill in your own example here), then I'll do what I've always dreamed of doing; one day I'll do what I love and I'll love what I'm doing.'

This way you can hopefully avoid ever having to sum up the courage it will take to make the break. In reality, of course, this excuse is a little like not having sex, but saving it all up for when you retire.

Be careful, however, if you have a real sense of purpose to what you do. If you are one of those people who have found out what you love to do and found someone to pay you to do it. If that's the case you can't help but be successful, or as Robert Benchley, the best-selling author, says: 'It took me 15 years to discover I had no talent for writing, but I couldn't give it up because by that time I was too famous.'

Exercise caution if you are someone who doesn't feel like they work for a living but instead play for a living. If you are so

EXERCISE CAUTION if you are someone who doesn't feel like they work for a living but instead play for a living.

passionate and absorbed by what you do that, if you had to, you'd happily pay someone else to let you do it. Be especially careful if you are your own boss.

D H Lawrence put it this way: 'There is no point in work unless it absorbs you, like an absorbing game. If it doesn't absorb you, it is never any fun. Don't do it.' That's fine coming from someone who just spent their time writing and loafing around. But it doesn't pay the mortgage, does it? If the above applies to your job or career, stop whatever you are doing at once and go back to being a wage slave doing something you hate for the rest of the days of your life. Anyway, what would you have to moan about if you didn't have a lousy job and a no-good boss?

Action not to take

Don't think about what job would make you leap out of bed each morning.

Don't think about how you can turn your hobby into your job.

Don't think about what you would work at if you didn't have to work.

Don't think about what really absorbs you. Don't ask yourself, 'What am I doing when I feel most alive?'

Don't answer the question, 'What do you feel is your greatest natural ability?' If you can't help answering it, don't stop to look at who you have been rather than sticking just to what you have done.

Don't think back to what you loved doing at seven years of age. Recent research indicates that successful adults often do something as a living that they enjoyed doing, and were good at, as a kid. So perhaps the Jesuits were right after all – give me the boy until he is seven and I'll give you the man.

Don't think what you would dare do if you knew you couldn't fail.

Step four

Don't know what you value in life (and if you do, lose sight of it).

Quote to avoid

'How different our lives are when we really know what is deeply important to us, and keeping that picture in mind, we manage ourselves each day to be and to do what really matters most.' **Stephen Covey**

In the first *Superman* movie, Lois Lane asks Superman what he stands for and, quick as a flash, he replies: 'Truth, justice and the American way.' We might not agree with his values but boy was he clear about what he stood for and what mattered most to him (besides, of course, the right to wear your underpants on the out-side). Do you know your values? Do you know what you stand for? Do you know what matters most to you in your working life and at home? I hope not. Values drive how we feel about the things we do, before, during and after we do them. So if you are unclear about your values, you can make terrible decisions about what you should and shouldn't do in life and business.

Values should drive all your behaviour at work. Here is Amazon.com's company motto:

Work hard. Have fun. Make history.

Can you see how that shows anyone at Amazon how to behave? They only need to ask: 'Am I working hard, having fun or making history right now? If not, then why am I doing it?'

You'd find the solution to most of your problems would be a return to your true values. Still, if you haven't a clue what your values are in the first place, you can be optimistic that your problems will remain.

A way to think about your values is as those emotions, moods or states you most enjoy being in, most of the time. So it stands to reason, if you are to enjoy maximum job dissatisfaction and the worst possible home life, you'd better remain unclear about what's most important to you and avoid any surroundings where your values will be satisfied.

A WAY TO THINK about your values is as those emotions, moods or states you most enjoy being in, most of the time.

What's more, most people have an endless set of rules of what needs to happen for them to feel a certain way. For instance, if I said to someone, 'What would need to happen for you to feel happy?' they might reply, 'When I'm earning £200,000 a year . . . when I can go through a week or longer with everyone being nice to me . . . when I buy something expensive like a car . . . when I win something unexpected like the lottery . . . when everybody returns my phone calls on time . . .'

Can you see how this person has set up the rules of life so they can rarely, if ever, win? Whereas contented, happy people have consciously set up the game with rules that make it as easy as possible for them to enjoy desirable emotions and rules that make it as difficult as possible for them to experience undesirable emotions. A client of mine, David, recently had a heart attack at a very young age. If you ask him what it now takes for him to feel happy he says just one thing – waking up above ground. Still, unless you've had a health scare, you can't live by this one simple rule for happiness, can you?

Action not to take

Don't decide what your five most important values in life and work are. Don't specify the rules, or conditions, you've determined which will easily allow you to feel each of these emotions. Don't make all your decisions based on your values.

Step five
Don't spend any of your time in the future.

Quote to avoid

'Never let your memories be greater than your dreams.' **Doug Ivester**

You'd never dream of jumping into a taxi and when the driver asked you, 'Where would you like to go?' saying, 'I don't know, just take me anywhere.' Yet this is a perfect metaphor for how most people lead their lives. I'll prove it to you. If I was to ask, 'Where will you be in five years' time?' you probably don't have a clue. That's because only 10% of the population are future focused. This means 90% of us are stuck in the now or the past. When someone says, 'Never mind five years from now, I don't even know where I'll be five minutes from now. I can't think about the future,' it is literally true. They can't think about the future because they don't believe, deep down, they have any influence over it. Most folks accept, without question, that they are victims of circumstances not creators of circumstances. And so should you. I mean, what is the point of thinking about the future when it's largely a matter of luck? Successful people, on the other hand, are visionaries. They don't believe in luck. They are in the driving seat of their own life and aren't content to be a passenger. They put themselves at cause, not effect.

As we said earlier, successful individuals and organizations know that everything is created twice. They know you must clearly see your future success in your mind's eye before you can create it in reality. They vividly imagine the successful completion of their goal, over and over again, until it becomes so familiar to them that as far as their unconscious mind is concerned they have already achieved it. These are the peak performers. Unfortunately, most people vividly imagine what they don't want. There is a name for this: worry. Both the good and the bad news is that you become what you think about most of the time. So, to speed up the failure process, don't be very careful what you think about! (More on this in steps twenty-eight and twenty-nine.)

When people first come on board a work-shop we run on a boat (yes, a boat), they often ask: 'Where is the boat sailing to?' Just for a laugh, I reply: 'I have absolutely no idea.' Actually, I know exactly our destination, but you see there are lots of people on boats, called their lives, who don't know where they are sailing to. They don't have a big engine on their boat called vision, values, purpose and goals. Which means they can't celebrate success because they'll never know when they've arrived. Plus, if they were to encounter a storm whilst at sea, without an engine, they could end up anywhere. Now it could be a nice harbour. However, if you can't see where you are going, there's a greater chance you're bound for the rocks or the bottom of the sea. Of course, if you don't put an engine on your boat, you are unlikely even to set sail in the first place. This will guarantee that you, like so many other great failures, will stay where you are for most, if not all, of your life. Nice thought.

WHERE ARE YOU SAILING TO?

Don't ever, ever, ever do the following powerful exercise.

Find some quiet, relaxing time with a loved one or colleague. Decide who, out of the two of you, is going to listen first. Your job once the exercise starts is to listen to the other person. This isn't a dialogue. The other person needs to do most of the talking. You need to show you are doing most of the listening. At times you may want to ask a question to clarify or understand further what the other person has said. That's OK. Just don't take over. You'll get your chance to do the talking later. Once the person you are listening to runs out of things to say, change roles. You talk and the other person now listens. What will you be talking about? You'll be talking about all your achievements in the last two years. Now before you start thinking, 'I don't have any achievements,' let me explain. I'm not talking about winning the gold medal. Getting out of bed regularly, on time, counts.

Plus don't just think about your achievements at work. What about all those other hats you wear? What about your achievements as a wife, husband, boyfriend or girlfriend, dad or mother? What about pastimes and hobbies? What achievements do you have to be proud of in all the areas of your life?

Now just before you start, there is a little switch. For the purpose of the exercise I'd like you to imagine it is now two years from

WHAT ABOUT your

achievements

as a wife, husband, boyfriend or girlfriend, dad or mother?

today. Imagine you've just been catapulted through time and space to two years in the future. Which means you are going to be talking about stuff that hasn't happened yet. The crucial thing is that you are going to talk about it as if it has. So it's important to stick to the past tense.

Now if I was listening to you, some of my questions might be:

➡ 'Where did you go on holiday (in two years from now) and did you have a good time?'

➡ 'Where are you living now (it's two years from now) and who with?' – be careful if you are doing this exercise with your partner.

➡ 'How has your career progressed in the last two years? Are you still working at the same place, doing the same thing?' – be careful if you are doing this exercise with your boss.

Once you've finished, here are some observations to consider:

When was the last time you did that then?

The usual answer is never. We are all perhaps used to traditional blue skies business planning where we look from now towards some date in the future and talk about what we might or might not do. What makes this exercise different, and more powerful, is that we are looking back. It brings an extra dimension that is usually absent when thinking about the future. And that's your emotions. Because you were talking about what you've already done and achieved, your emotions become involved. If you don't get excited talking about this stuff, when are you going to get excited?

Go do it with someone else

Two or more people with a shared vision are like an unstoppable train.

Do this exercise with your team. Better still, do it with your significant other.

Did you quickly run out of things to say?

This might mean you aren't future oriented enough. Remember 90% of the population spend all their time in the present and the past. Maybe you need to plan to spend more time thinking about the future.

How clear was your vision?

If I'd been listening to you and you were telling me about this fantastic new house you now live in (now it's two years from today), I'd have asked, 'What colour is the front door?' 'How many rooms does it have?' 'What plants do you have in the garden?' You can only realize your vision to the extent that you can clearly see, hear and feel it. Athletes at the Olympics didn't sort of, vaguely, kind of see themselves winning the race. When they mentally rehearsed the events they saw everything in absolute, specific, clear detail.

Discover what not to do

This exercise is also good for giving you ideas on what not to do. Maybe you found yourself telling your partner about some long-held goal, dream or ambition. For example, maybe you talked about that book you said you were always going to write and have now written. Maybe you said it's even now on sale in all good bookshops. But if, as you talked about it, you didn't get really excited, are you really going to make it happen? Sometimes what we thought we really wanted turns out to be something we don't really care enough about. We simply don't have enough enthusiasm and energy to make it happen. Forget it.

So don't practise back-from-the-future thinking. Don't think about what success will look, feel and sound like five years from now (yes, it's even more effective to think five years from now rather than just a piddling two).

While you are at it, don't think about letting go of the past either. Don't stop trying to fix or solve past mistakes. Don't merely make peace with what's happened and move on. Just continue to wallow in things you can't change. Knowing you tried, and letting it go, may be exactly what you need to make the current situation acceptable again. Doing this would also release the extra energy you might need to design your future life rather then let it unfold by accident.

Oh, and to complete your misery, don't be in the now or enjoy the moment. Many people squander the present yearning for a better future. You might like to join them. Finally, I should point out that you will find it is impossible to reach a future goal anyway if your present is not set up to support it.

Step six
Don't have any goals.

Quote to avoid

'An average person with average talents and ambition and average education can outstrip the most brilliant genius in our society if that person has clear, focused goals.' **Brian Tracy**

A mate of mine, Phil, has achieved lots of goals. He's done things he's always dreamed of doing. But that wasn't always the case. Phil, for as long as he can remember, had a deep desire to visit New Zealand. That's because when he was very young his aunt and uncle emigrated there and, after an emotional goodbye, Phil thought, 'I must visit them one day.' But just like with the vast majority of the population, that's all that it remained – a one-day wish.

Then two things happened. Firstly, Phil was shown a way of setting goals that was simple but seemed to work. It called for him to put his goals in writing. Phil wanted to know why that was important. The explanation was that until you crystallize your goals, until you define them clearly, they will always remain vague wishes, dreams and fantasies. Phil had to make some choices based on the time-management law of 'the excluded alternative', which states that if you are doing one thing you can't, by definition, be doing something else. He was also given another reason for putting his goals in writing and that was to bring to bear the power of his unconscious mind. Phil had learned that by deciding what he wanted, then putting it down in writing, it became stored in his unconscious. This meant, even when he was sleeping, his unconscious mind was figuring out ways to help him achieve his goals.

That's why if you were to follow the system for writing goals that Phil learnt, then took those written goals and put them where you wouldn't see them for exactly 12 months, something remarkable would happen. Twelve months later, if you were to take out those goals and review them, you would discover, on average, that you had achieved 80% of them. And all you consciously did was write them in a certain way. Your unconscious took care of the rest. How does that work? 'Who cares?' says Phil. 'It just does.' (More about this in the next step.)

Plus, by having written goals, Phil increased the level of synchronicity[1] that occurred. People with goals will tell you that meaningful coincidences occur all the time. Or as Johann Wolfgang von Goethe,[2] the German polymorph (amongst other things he was the author of *Faust*, a philosopher, a general and an ice skater), would put it: 'Until one is committed, there is always hesitancy, the chance to draw back, always ineffectiveness. Concerning all acts of initiative (and creation) there is one elementary truth, the ignorance of which kills countless ideas and splendid plans: that the moment one definitely commits oneself, then providence moves too. All sorts of things occur to help one that would not otherwise have occurred. A whole stream of events issue from the decision raising in one's favour all manner

---

[1] Synchronicity – a fancy word for meaningful coincidences. In other words, it's where you have a specific need and the timing is right. Successful people say that if you keep a journal of the number of times meaningful coincidences occur, you will begin to notice that they occur more and more. It's a simple way to speed up your success rate dramatically, so don't invest in a journal.

[2] As well as being good at loads of things and generally giving Leonardo da Vinci a run for his money, Goethe still holds a mental world record, even though he has been dead for several hundred years. Goethe's record is for the biggest ever written vocabulary. For example, the average person, with an average education, will have a written vocabulary of around 12,000 words. William Shakespeare used 25,000 different written words. But get this, Goethe had a written vocabulary of over 50,000 individual words. Now why is this important? When I first heard it I thought, imagine being at a party with Goethe, you wouldn't understand a word he said. The point is, vocabulary is still used as a classic test of intelligence; words are ideas. Quite simply, by combining a vast number of words Goethe could have profound thoughts and ideas that would never occur to us. That's why many successful people I've met say Goethe, with his huge intelligence and outstanding achievements in so many different fields, is worth paying careful attention to.

of unforeseen incidents and meetings and material assistance which no man could have dreamt would come his way.'

You see, Goethe thought that the opportunities, and the people who could help you, were always there – it's just that you didn't see them before. Thousands of opportunities probably passed you by without you even realizing it. Neuroscience explains why this phenomenon occurs. The Reticular Activating System (or RAS) within the brain acts as a filter to how you experience the world. Current thinking says we are exposed to over two million pieces, some say even more, of sensory information per second. Obviously if we tried consciously to process all of that information, our brains would explode and smoke would come out of our ears. Instead we can be consciously aware of only a few pieces of information at any one time. As for the rest, unless something brings it to our attention we will be blissfully unaware of it. For instance, if you were to stop reading for a moment and think about your left foot and whether it is comfortable inside your shoe, where was that piece of information until I brought it to your attention? Well, unless your foot was already hurting, the answer is nowhere: things were being looked after on an unconscious level. Now, when you set a goal – say to own a particular make and model of car – this is programmed into your RAS. Which is why it suddenly appears that you can't go anywhere without seeing your car, the roads are positively groaning under

THOUSANDS OF opportunities

probably passed you by

without you

even realizing it.

the number of them. So what happened? Did everyone suddenly go out and buy the exact car you were wanting, or were that number of cars there all the time? It was your RAS that got you to sit up and take notice.

Another significant thing that happened to convince Phil about the power of goal setting was when someone challenged his belief about what was possible. He'd always used the excuse that, as a company director, he couldn't take five weeks off work to visit New Zealand. Then someone said (as it happened, it was my sister): 'What would happen if you did?' It turned out that once he asked, his fellow directors said it would be fine. Now all he needed was the money . . . but that's another story.

Action not to take

Can you see why it's vital that you don't do what Phil did? Don't take time really to crystallize what you want to achieve, just leave it as a vague, 'one day I'll get round to it' dream. Because if you do, you'll bring the mighty laser-like focus of the RAS to bear.

Don't, for one moment, believe it's possible for you to do it or that you deserve it.

Someone, possibly Mark Twain,[3] once said: 'We are not human doings, we are human beings.' So if you do slip into goal setting, don't start by first having goals about what you want to be before you set goals about what you want to do and have.

---

[3] Throughout this guide where I can't find the source of a quote I'll assume it was Mark Twain. Just so you'll have another factual inaccuracy to complain about when it turns out that it wasn't him after all.

Step seven

If you do have goals, don't put them in writing, and if you do, don't think too big.

Quote to avoid

'A study conducted by David Jensen at UCLA covering a broad range of people from every walk of life concluded that people who set goals and develop a plan of action to reach them are happier and healthier, earn considerably more money, and get along better with the people at home than do people who have no clearly defined objectives. Consider this happiness factor as you set your goals.'

Zig Ziglar

Ever heard of the study done with Harvard graduates? In the 1950s graduates were asked how many had goals. The answer was almost everyone (you'd have to be dead from the neck up not to have some goals, dreams and ambitions). More important, the students were then asked how many had put those goals in writing. The answer was only 3%. After following them around for the next 30 years (which must have been annoying if you were one of the graduates), it was found that 3% of the group were worth more financially than the other 97% combined! It was the same 3% who had written goals. Coincidence? The point is, as long as goals stay in your head they will stay only dreams.

Another reason why students of failure must be careful not to commit their goals to ink is that it makes you think. You see, you can't have everything (there isn't enough time to have everything, anyway where would you keep it all?) but you can have anything. Most people just won't decide what their anything is going to be. Remember, success is a decision. All you have to decide is what you want to be, do and have. Rather than make some tough choices about how they would like to spend their time, failures put it off, hoping they can realize all the dreams swirling around inside their head. That's until they wake up one day and realize time has run out.

Over 50 years of research, not just from Harvard but also from areas like Neuro Linguistic Programming,[1] proves that having any written goal will get you into the top 3%. However, if you want to reach the top 1%, and this is confirmed by my own direct experience of working with hundreds of individuals, you also need to write your goals to meet some strict criteria. That's why all of Phil's goals are written as SMARTS:

> ➡ **Specific and Simple**
> Define exactly what you want to accomplish. Focus, laser-like, on just one thing. The simpler you can make it, the better your brain will like it and act on it.
>
> ➡ **Measurable and Meaningful to you**
> Cost, quantity, quality, number, percentage – think of all the ways you can measure your progress. You must be able to say whether you 'did' or 'didn't' do it. Make sure the goal has meaning for you and is going to make a difference to you and your life.
>
> ➡ **Achievable, As if now and Realistic[2]**
> Think of something within reach but just out of your grasp. This will be up to you. What seems achievable and realistic to you may not be to someone else. If you don't believe you can

▶

---

[1] NLP – not the most catchy name for what is a very powerful and rapid way to create positive change in your life. It's not all beards and sandals. Honest. NLP is based on three simple principles for success. Firstly – know what you want; have a clear idea of your outcome in any situation. Secondly – be alert and keep your senses open so that you can notice what you are getting. Thirdly – have the flexibility to keep changing what you do until you get what you want.

[2] See Disclaimers at back of guide.

do it, you won't. The 'A' also stands for writing the goal 'As if now'. By writing the goal as though you've already achieved it, in the present tense, using sensory adjectives (for example, I feel and look great now I'm a size . . .), every time you read it your emotions, your unconscious mind and your Reticular Activating System will get involved in its accomplishment.

➡ **Timed and Toward**

Set a deadline. Analyze where you are now in relation to the goal and then measure how long you will reasonably need to complete the goal. Be careful not to limit yourself by setting the deadline too far in the future. It may be possible to achieve a goal much quicker than you thought. How long did it take someone else to achieve a similar thing? Maybe, if you learn from them, you could do it even quicker. However, a goal that's set too close can be more demotivating than motivating. It's a question of finding the right balance. There is no such thing as an unrealistic goal, just an unrealistic deadline. Phil says sometimes he has achieved things so quickly, that he beats the deadline he set for himself by miles. Other things which he expected to have happened by now, he is still waiting for. In the latter case, Phil just asks himself: 'Is this still a worthy goal?' If the answer is 'yes', and often with the benefit of more accurate knowledge available to him since his first attempt, he just resets the deadline. Also make sure your goal is towards motivated. That you are driven by something you want rather than something you don't want.

➡ **Step**

Get the last step. Get really clear about what evidence you will need to prove you did it. What will you see, hear and feel when you have achieved it? If you don't do this, often you will fall short just before you might have achieved your goal. For instance, let's say your goal is to move into a new house. What would the last step be? Would it be the 'sold' sign in the garden? The estate agent handing you the keys? Or your family and friends joining you at the housewarming party? Which would best tell you that you have achieved your goal? Once you've decided, always write your SMARTS goal to encompass this last step.

Phil then checked he had the intense desire to achieve the goal, that he had a compelling, motivating reason for wanting it. He knew this would greatly enhance his chances of success.

That's why he gave more thought to the why than he did to the how. He knew if he had a big enough why then he could, must, find the how. If you have got a really good reason, you can make yourself do almost anything. (If you have failed to achieve a goal in the past it may be because you simply didn't have enough reasons.)

Phil then identified the obstacles he needed to overcome; identified the help he would need; planned his priorities; got a clear mental picture, or dominant thought pattern, of the goal already accomplished; and finally backed his plan with commitment, persistence and resolve. And he believed he could do it.

Oh, and one other crucial thing – having done all of the above, Phil took action.

Phil says sometimes a small, easily achievable goal can dramatically change things – say the quality of a relationship. This gave me food for thought. It occurred to me that I had something that I shared with my oldest son, Tom (we are both passionate about our local rugby team, Leeds Rhinos, and go and watch them together), but that there wasn't anything that I and my other son, Finlay, did together – our 'thing' if you like. So, just by way of an experiment you understand, I set a goal to find something. As soon as I did that, suddenly everywhere I looked, I kept seeing and reading about Games Workshop. I'd never noticed it before but seemingly it's been around for years (there goes that RAS again). This is a hobby with masses of appeal to boys, and for that matter, men. You collect, build and paint model soldiers and then stage battles. So for a few years this became our thing and something we could share. It proved a brilliant way of strengthening our relationship. This all happened when Finlay was nine since which, unlike several men I know, he's moved on from Games Workshop. Now, at the time of writing, one of the things we share is reading the same books. This means I get to read one of Finlay's favourites like 'Mortal Engines' by Philip Reeve and he gets to read one of mine like 'To Kill A Mockingbird' by Harper Lee. It's still a shared experience and it gives us loads to talk about and debate. This, if you've got a teenage son who normally communicates with caveman grunts, is a very worthwhile outcome. Of course I wouldn't suggest you should set yourself these sorts of small goals that can create big results.

After discovering this stuff works, Phil now also feels there is even more magic in thinking big. He agrees with the advice of Les Brown and Mark Victor Hansen who said: 'Shoot for the moon. Even if you miss it you will land among the stars' and 'Think big, act big and set out to accomplish big results.' Or as Donald Trump puts it: 'If you are going to be thinking anyway, you might as well think big.' So remember, please don't write down your goals and don't think big. That's assuming you give the quality of your life any thought at all.

Action not to take

Don't join the 3% of people who design their life rather than go with the flow. (Hear that noise up ahead? Sounds like rapids to me.) Don't think big. Be modest, never think: 'If not you, who? If not now, when?'

Don't make the distinction between outcome goals and perform-ance goals. For example, in athletics an outcome goal might be to win a gold medal whereas a performance goal might be to

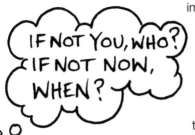

improve your time by two seconds. If all your goals are very, very outcome focused you might feel stuck and get despondent. Forget the purpose of goal setting is to feel motivated and to enjoy the process not just the end result. The big difference between an outcome goal and a performance goal is that a performance goal is within your control.

THE BIG difference between

an outcome goal and

a performance goal

is that a performance goal is within

your control.

Have you noticed that when you want something too badly, when it matters so much, you can get so wrapped up in it that you can't see anything else? This makes you very uptight and affects your performance. Instead of pulling the goal towards you, you end up pushing it away. Just bring to mind an important job interview. You wanted the job so badly, you weren't yourself and as a result you blew it. Or as Chinese philosopher Chuang Tzu says: 'When an archer is shooting for nothing, he has all his skills, when he is shooting for a prize, the prize divides him, he cares, he thinks more about winning than shooting and the need drains him of his power.' Don't do what successful people do, which is to develop the ability to walk the fine line between taking action and being detached, to leave it alone, get out of the way and enjoy life.

Step eight
Don't plan your priorities.

Quote to avoid

'If you wish to know your past life, look to your present circumstances. If you wish to know of your future life, look to your present actions.' **Buddhist saying**

Two factors drive how we spend our time. First there are those things that are Urgent – which is best described as the feeling of 'I must do it now' (tense, pressured, some might say exhilarating). Then there are those things that are Important – these are activities that contribute significantly to our goals and have a

FIG 3 Where do you spend most of your time?

long-term impact. Knowing this we can now categorize time and our activities in four ways:

1. Fire fighting (Urgent and Important)

This is the category where you are constantly reacting to what's going on. Stuff that you didn't plan for, that's got to be done now. Irate clients, phones ringing, people walking into your office and resigning out of the blue, crying children, heart surgery, crisis. Because you don't take time to prioritize, you are mostly reactive, driven by the tyranny of the urgent. By the way, some of the best fire fighters are also some of the best arsonists. They are so addicted to the buzz of the urgent, and like to be seen as stepping in and saving things at the last possible moment, that they often start the fires in the first place.

2. Fire prevention (Important not Urgent)

The category of quality. The more time you spend in here the less time you'll need to spend in category 1. Activities in here include things to do with the long term such as planning, innovation, vision, training and even physical exercise. This is where you can head things off at the pass before they become critical and move over to category 1. The things in here don't act on us, we have to

BY THE WAY, some of the
best fire fighters are also some of **the best** arsonists.

act on them. All these activities can be put off so we have to make ourselves do them. But seeing that, on average, you'll be interrupted every nine minutes, there's fat chance of that.

3. False alarms (Urgent not Important)

This is the category of deception. It feels just like category 1. You are fooled by the noise of urgency. For example, people running into your office and screaming in a high-pitched voice that 'we've got a problem' creates the illusion that this is important when in reality it's only urgent. And usually just to them.

4. Fire escape (Not Important not Urgent)

Escape activities like idle chat and trips to the coffee machine. Doing anything rather than what needs doing. It's nice here, isn't it?

Action not to take

Here's how that clever clogs Goethe, who we last heard from in step six, summed it up: 'Things that matter most should never be at the mercy of things that matter least.' Or in other words, your priorities determine your progress. So, if we don't listen to a dead German philosopher's advice, in which of the above categories shouldn't you plan to spend most of your time if you are to avoid achieving anything worthwhile?

Don't think of your life as like designing and building a house. What structure would it have? How many and what types of rooms? Where would you put them in your design? You might have a work room. How big would it be and how much time would you spend there? You might have a family room, a play room and even a bar. Where? How big? How much time spent in each? Don't ponder these questions, just get to the end of your life and realize you spent too much of it hanging out in all the wrong places.

If you do have a dream, goal or ambition, don't make a list of all, or any, actions you can take to achieve it. Working back from your final outcome, don't figure out the main steps you need to take before you can achieve your goal and write them down. Don't take at least one small step a day based on your priorities.

Step nine
Don't involve other people.

Quote to avoid

You can have everything in life you want if you'll just help enough other people to get what they want! **Zig Ziglar (yes, it's the guy with the funny name again)**

You go into work one day and meet John (names have been changed to protect the guilty). You say, 'Hi John, how are you?' John replies, 'Fine,' to which you have to respond, 'Well, will you tell your face?' The thing is not only do you become what you think about most of the time (see step twenty-eight), but you also become who you spend most of your time with. Thinking about your family, friends and associates for a moment: what are they like? Here is a less than exhaustive list of some of the characteristics of an utter failure in life, work and everything:

➡ lots of moaning;

➡ frequent sighing;

➡ extremely low self-esteem;

➡ lacking any form of enthusiasm;

➡ no self-belief;

➡ spots and greasy hair (a bit of artistic licence here but that's what they would look like if their bodies matched their minds);

➡ pessimistic;

➡ lousy values, lousy vision, no sense of purpose, no goals;

➡ scared and/or jealous of success;

➡ blaming everything, and everyone, apart from themselves, for what they are, do and have.

Look, this list could go on and on, you get the idea, so let's stop now, before I become too dejected.

Now, if you were to list the names of those people you spend most of your time with, how would each one score against the above out of ten? Scary eh? It's hardly surprising you're deeply depressed. So don't stop hanging around with this gang, they'll help sabotage your success at every turn. If you do go off and try to do something different or new, most of your current mates will see it as a threat. Which is why you can't expect their support.

Dr Wayne Dyer believes that whether we live in Borneo or Birmingham, everyone belongs to a tribe. Every tribe operates to certain guidelines, customs and cultural norms. Some ensure the tribe's survival, but many can hold the gifted individual back. Here is how Dr Dyer puts it: 'Let go of the idea that the tribe is going to give approval. When you're learning anything that is outside the parameters of the tribe, what you are doing is saying, "I am going to evolve at a faster rate". But if you go to the tribe and tell them that, immediately you're going to be put in your place. The mantra of the tribe is, "But what will people think?" The speed of the tribe is slow.'

However, I've noticed that successful people deliberately associate with other successful people. They seek out the pacemakers – people who are moving as quickly, probably even quicker, than they are. People who will challenge their thinking about what is possible. They create what you might call a Master Mind Group. They understand the cumulative power of several minds. In Napoleon Hill's classic book *Think and Grow Rich*, a whole chapter is about the benefits – both financial and emotional – of creating and using a Master Mind Group. It makes sense to combine the power of several minds to solve problems, develop strategies and achieve results. But there are more advantages to it than that. As Hill wrote: 'No two minds ever come together without, thereby, creating a third, invisible, intangible force which may be likened to a third mind.'

Action not to take

Don't stop listening to the opinions of other people who, although they have achieved nothing with their lives, still feel qualified to pass on their wisdom to you. When your existing pals or relatives say you can't do something, that it is impossible, don't be tempted to quote Nelson Mandela back at them: 'Our deepest fear is not that we are inadequate. Our deepest fear is that we are powerful beyond measure. It is our light, not our darkness, that most frightens us. We ask ourselves, Who am I to be brilliant, gorgeous, talented, fabulous? Actually, who are you not to be? Your playing small doesn't serve the world. There's nothing enlightened about shrinking so that other people won't feel insecure around you. As we let our own light shine, we unconsciously give other people permission to do the same. As we're liberated from our own fear, our presence automatically liberates others.'

Of course, you probably can't be bothered to remember all that. The easy alternative is to state, 'I don't believe you.' Over and over again. This is what Nelson did every time he was told that the mighty apartheid system couldn't be destroyed by one man sitting in a prison cell. You mustn't make this your replacement mantra for the more popular 'But what would people think?' crowd pleaser.

Don't identify a group of people whom you admire, whose coat tails you can cling to or shoulders you can stand on. People who can help you achieve your goals and you can help achieve theirs. Don't commit to meeting and communicating on a regular basis to swap ideas and offer encouragement.

Step ten
Don't have a mentor or be a mentor.

Quote to avoid

' The fragrance always stays in the hand that gives the rose. ' **Hada Bejar**

Besides seeking out Master Mind Alliances, successful people also identify one or two individuals who can become their personal mentors. Someone perhaps, but not always, in the same field as them. Someone, often but not always, older and more experienced. Someone who is already achieving the results they'd like to enjoy. To identify the right person they ask themselves questions based on the goals they are trying to achieve. Questions like, 'What resources will I need?' 'What do I have now?' 'Do I know or can I find anyone who has ever done this before?'

They then search out the best person to help. They encourage themselves with this startling fact: you are only, at the most, six people away from meeting anyone on the planet! That's right, as amazing as it seems, you're only six moves from being able to pick the brains of anyone you care to mention, famous and not so famous. This is based on what's called 'six degrees of separation'. Scientists discovered, originally by studying the action of thousands of ball bearings, that one individual ball bearing could connect with any other in six moves or less. They then wondered if the same principle could be applied to human relationships (well, that's scientists for you). They found that it could. For example, I know someone, who knows someone, who knows someone, who knows someone who is friends with Bill Clinton. So if you knew me, you'd only be six people away from Bill (I'm not even going to speculate on what you might want to ask him). Now, of course, you'd have to know the right six people. But if you think about the mighty power of the Internet, how hard can it be to get personal advice from anyone on earth?

IF YOU THINK about the **mighty power** of the Internet, **how hard can it be** to get personal advice from anyone **on earth?**

Well, the answer is quite hard if you approach it from just selfishly thinking about what's in it for you. So that's what you should do. If you just approach them with your begging bowl, whining that you would really appreciate their help, giving no thought to what's in it for them, that should ensure they'll never, ever speak to you again. These are busy people, so the more you can waste their valuable time the better. You must never ask, 'How can I deserve their support?'

Anyway, there are zero benefits to being a mentor, aren't there? I'm currently mentoring a couple of people who want to be professional public speakers. I've lost count of the times they've asked me very detailed questions about my strategies for getting on in this business. It's strange because I often tell them to do certain things, then realize I've stopped doing those things myself and must get back to doing them. Or they'll discover something incredible that I don't do, perhaps from talking to another mentor, and tell me all about it. How annoying is that?

Action not to take

Don't ever agree to mentor someone on the understanding that they mentor someone else.

Step eleven

Don't get advice from people you've never met or who are dead.

Quote to avoid

'*If I have seen farther than others, it is because I was standing on the shoulders of giants.*' **Isaac Newton**

I've spent years around many successful individuals and organizations that, if you want to remain a failure, I strongly recommend you stay away from (I did it purely for the purposes of research you understand). For example, as a professional speaker, I'm often on stage with well-known and prosperous entrepreneurs. It just can't be avoided. The conclusion I've come to is that, without exception, they are all stark staring mad. Not only do they have beliefs about life and business that are wildly different to the majority of the population, like there's no such thing as failure, but they also take advice from dead people. That's right. When faced with a problem, or opportunity, they often ask one of their heroes from history for advice. If they wanted the advice of someone sparky and extremely positive, they might consult with Mozart, who has been described as a pathological optimist. How, you may be wondering, do they communicate with Mozart? (Who, just in case you missed the news, has been dead for a couple of hundred years. 'It is sobering to consider that when Mozart was my age he had already been dead for a year' – Tom Lehrer.) The answer is that they talk to him inside their heads – told you these people were crazy. The theory is that although they know, in reality, they are simply talking to themselves, because of their in-depth knowledge of Mozart, his

personality and his life, they can come up with new insights and solutions filtered through his unique point of view. Now, imagine if you started consulting with a similar Master Mind Group of your own, what that might do to your thinking. So don't do it.

I OFTEN ASK HIM FOR ADVICE

As well as talking to dead people, successful folk also seek advice from people they don't know but know of. Having asked them how they do this, typically the answer is that, over the years, they have built up a vast library of success. Try this for yourself. Find any successful person and ask them, 'Do you have a library?' They almost always say 'yes'. Then ask them, 'What kinds of books are in your library?' and they'll tell you mostly biographies and autobiographies of successful people. Rather than invent the wheel, what these people do is model success. By the way, if they live in a big house, with a big library, ask them, 'Which came first, the books or the library?' and they'll usually tell you it was reading the books that enabled them to afford the library.

So remember, when you are unsure of something, don't ask for advice, especially from dead people. Still, can I ask your advice? Have you any idea why the number of this step isn't pronounced onety one?

Action not to take

Don't talk to your heroes dead or alive. Don't buy biographies or autobiographies of people who have led successful lives. Don't seek advice from the most likely, and unlikely, sources. For instance, here is a piece of wisdom from Rosemary, aged seven: 'Never try to hide a piece of broccoli in a glass of milk.'

Step twelve
Don't take action right now.

Quote to avoid

'You can't build a reputation on what you are going to do.' **Henry Ford**

Someone once said: 'There are two ways to reach the top of an oak tree – you climb it or sit on an acorn and wait.' It's really important you don't do anything. Don't even lift a finger in the direction of your ambitions. Just keep hoping something will turn up, even though someone else said: 'People who wait for something to turn up might start with their own shirt sleeves.'

Never mind all that *carpe diem*, seize the day, stuff. I mean, you've got all the time in the world, haven't you? Let's put it off till tomorrow. For instance, let's say the average person reading this is only 35 years of age, then you've a good chance of living to be at least 80 (although remember, pessimists die younger, so you might have to take that into account). Now we're told in a life-time the average person will spend 23 years sleeping, 14 years sitting in sofas or armchairs, $4\frac{1}{2}$ years eating, 2 years in the bath, 2 years reading newspapers and 30 seconds making love. So that leaves loads of time, doesn't it? Indeed, why not delay things indefinitely? The fact is, few people have developed a real sense of urgency, apart from New York cab drivers, so why should you? No matter that Jonathan Winters says: 'I couldn't wait for success, so I went ahead without it.'

It would seem there is a direct relationship between how fast you act and results. Tony Robbins, one of those sunny American motivational gurus, says: 'Never leave the site of a goal without

IT WOULD SEEM there is
a direct relationship
between how fast you act and
results.

taking some kind of action.' I think what he means is, as soon as you've written the goal, ask yourself: 'What can I do right now to help me achieve it?' That might just be a phone call to someone who can give you advice. As usual you should ignore the wisdom of these world-renowned experts. This shouldn't be too difficult because here are some universal truths:

➡ You always secretly feel a bit scared when stroking a horse.

➡ Driving through tunnels makes people feel excited.

➡ The most painful household accident involves stepping on an upturned electrical plug in bare feet; a close second is walking on a Lego brick.

➡ No one respects a man who carries a dog.

➡ People who can't drive always slam passenger doors too hard.

➡ After all is said, more is said than done.

So just keep talking about what you are going to do but don't do it. Your goal isn't to get moving, to take enthusiastic action, right this second. Your goal isn't to become unstoppable. Your goal is to be the same, do the same and have the same as everyone else, which you've got to admit, isn't very much. Of course, if you can, aim for even less than the average. Anyway, why worry? You know you're not willing to take action, because just like most people, you are intrinsically lazy. A Zen master observed another universal truth when he said: 'After the ecstasy, the laundry.' You simply don't want to put in the work necessary to be an outstanding success. Please don't keep reading this rubbish – just stare blankly into space and do nothing.

Action not to take

Here is a riddle for you:

Five frogs are sitting on a log.

Four decide to jump off.

How many are left?

Answer: Five.

Why?

Because deciding and doing are not the same thing.

Don't think about what you would do, how you would change your life, if you won £1 million cash today. Also, don't think about what you would do, how you would spend your time, if you learned today that you had only six months to live (by the way, successful people don't wait for these things to happen before they act on their dreams). If the answers to these thoughts do pop into your mind, I know that being a scaredy-pants you wouldn't change a thing, especially your job. Even though no one ever said on their death bed, 'I wish I'd spent more time at the office' or, 'At least I made budget.' Remember, action is everything, so don't act. Besides, unless you are prepared to act fast and furious, it's probably already too late, as Harry Emerson Fosdick says: 'The world is moving so fast these days that the man who says it can't be done is generally interrupted by someone doing it.'

Step thirteen
Don't get feedback on your actions.

Quote to avoid

' To learn anything other than the stuff you find in books, you need to be able to experiment, to make mistakes, to accept feedback and to try again. It doesn't matter whether you are learning to ride a bike or starting a new career, the cycle of experiment, feedback and new experiment is always there. '

Charles Handy

People often ask me, 'Have you ever got anything right the first time?' I can think of only three times. Each time my wife and I decided to try for a child. She got pregnant immediately, first time, every time. Still, I can't take credit for this because, at least on my behalf, it was only 30 seconds' work. Other than that most people aren't going to get it right even after their fortieth attempt.

According to business guru Tom Peters, it takes the Sony Corporation of Japan just five working days from having an idea about a new product to having something it can test in the marketplace. Guess how long it takes most companies? Tom says on average up to 11 months. Why? Because Sony isn't chasing perfection, it is just out to get some feedback which it can then build into its next attempt. Whereas the mantra that always goes up from the typical Western research and development department is: 'Oh, please, if you just gave us more time and more money this would be so much better. It'd be just perfect!' The thing is, even if you gave them all the time and money in the world, it still wouldn't be right. And you'd be waiting an eternity before you could find out whether customers liked what you'd got. It's a bit like the young lady who once asked me: 'Do you give private lessons in public speaking?'

Well, that's really going to work, isn't it? What are you going to do, practise in front of the mirror until you are perfect, then go and speak in front of a thousand people? No, you need to get out there and get feedback no matter how you've done, sooner rather than later, if it's going to be of any use.

Failure, remember, is an unconscious habit. How hard can it be to give up the first time you don't get what you want? So don't even think about trying some other approach. Just throw in the towel. Finally, remember that if you don't have a clearly defined outcome and no goals to aim for, you won't even get started in the first place.

HOW HARD can it be to give up the first time you don't get what you want?

Action not to take

'Losses aren't a waste of time. They are an apprenticeship,' says Greg Norman, the golfer. But what would he know about it? Don't buy into the belief that anything worth doing is worth doing badly at first.

Don't give yourself permission not to be perfect. Don't follow General Patton's advice when he said: 'A good plan violently executed is far better than a perfect plan carried out next week.' Instead insist it has to be right first and every time. And you are not going to act until it is. This level of perfectionism should keep you immobile for long periods of time.

Don't have any means of getting feedback. If someone accidentally gives you some feedback on what you've done, treat it as criticism and ignore it. Oh, and tell them to mind their own business in future. Of course not all feedback is constructive. This is how the playwright Samuel Beckett attempted to encourage an actor who lamented, 'I'm Failing'; Beckett said, 'Go on failing. Only next time, try to fail better.'

Step fourteen
Don't adjust.

Quote to avoid

‘It is common sense to take a method and try it. If it fails, admit it frankly and try another. But above all, try something.’ **Franklin D Roosevelt**

Here is a key thought. In fact, it's so important in this guide to failure that I'm going to underline it. So you never, ever forget it. And it's this: <u>Don't become a kid again</u>. Do you remember how curious you were as a kid? How experimental? How open to new ideas? How creative? As Freud put it: 'What a distressing contrast there is between the radiant curiosity of the child and the feeble mentality of the average adult.' Now he may have been a smart Alec, but he was right. Childlike behaviour can generate a massive number of successful results (in fact, you can best describe geniuses as big babies). Resist it at all costs.

DON'T BECOME ONE OF THESE

For example, here is how kids learn to walk. They get a role model (by the way another very dangerous thing for a student of failure to do – see step thirty-one) and watch the role model, ie an adult, getting around on just two legs. Then they copy them. And what happens first time they try to walk? That's right, they fall over. Now instead of being sensible and packing the whole idea in, being kids, and I guess being incredibly naïve about the ways of the world, they dust themselves down and have another go. And what happens? Right again. They fall over. And so on. The thing is, they keep adjusting and trying things out, like holding on to the furniture, until they succeed. Imagine if we treated our children in the way that most managers treat their staff. We'd be saying, 'I'm sorry Tom, you've had three goes at this learning to walk malarky and you've still not cracked it, so you are going to have to stop now and crawl around on your bottom for the rest of your life.' Which is why many adults you meet are still bottom crawlers, metaphorically speaking.

The 'law of requisite variety' originally comes from the world of quantum mechanics, so a fat lot of good it is to us. However, it states that the part of the system with the most flexibility ends up controlling the system. This law explains why kids always get what they want, eventually – 'please Mum, can we have a dog . . .' (now repeat 10,000 times). It also means if you can manage to lock yourself into your staid and fixed adult behaviour, and just do the same old things, over and over again, you will never get what you want. And that shouldn't be too hard, for as Lord Campbell said: 'The chains of habit are generally too small to be felt until they are too strong to be broken.'

So the chances of you developing more behavioural flexibility, at your age, are remote. Maybe Albert Einstein, the big baby, was right when he said: 'Only two things are infinite, the universe and human stupidity, and I'm not sure about the former.' In fact, to develop a new way of doing something until it becomes a habit, experts claim you'd have to persist at it for 21 consecutive days or even longer. I'm suggesting you don't, even for a moment, think about changing how you behave in order to achieve something. What's the point?

It's also hard to adjust if you don't know where you've got to in the first place. My wife Candy was queuing at the post office a little while ago. Whilst waiting she began talking to the lady next

I'M SUGGESTING you don't, even for a moment, think about changing how you behave in order to achieve something.

to her. She had a strong feeling that they'd met before but couldn't quite place where. Like lots of us in that situation, she was too embarrassed to ask directly the woman's name and where they knew each other from. Eventually, just to make conversation, Candy said: 'So, are you still living in the same place?' To which her companion replied: 'Yes, I'm still living next door to you.'

You don't want to be any more aware of what's going on around you than that. Don't turn up your senses to number 11 and notice the things others miss. Successful people are aware of the signals, both conscious and unconscious, that are being sent out by others. They are keen to notice if what they are doing is working. On the other hand, failures are like fish, or as Einstein also said: 'Fish will be the last to discover water.'

Action not to take

Remember, it's OK to want things (I don't want you to think that failures don't want things). Just don't do anything about the things you want. If you do take action, at the most try a couple of things.

Don't use your sensory acuity to spot what's working and what's not.

If you don't get what you want, don't keep adjusting your strategy until you do. Quit while you're ahead.

Step fifteen

Don't get even more feedback, don't be flexible . . . (you get the idea).

Quote to avoid

Rules for being human:
You will learn lessons.
There are no mistakes – only lessons.
A lesson is repeated until it is learned.
If you don't learn lessons, they get harder
(pain is one way the universe gets your attention).
You'll know you've learned a lesson when your actions change. **Anon**

Here's another law for you. The law of probability suggests that the more things we try, the more likely we are to succeed. I know, but what's the point of wanton experimentation? Yet some people just don't seem to be able to stop themselves. Do you know who are the most daring group of experimenters on the planet? I'll give you a clue: we've already talked about them, they're really small and they can demonstrate so much behavioural flexibility, in trying to reach their goals, it's frightening. That's right, kids. Do you remember when you were little, how crystal-clear you were about what you wanted, and how determined, come what may, that you were going to have it? Take that bar of chocolate. Strategy one would be to ask sweetly whether you could have it. When that didn't work, strategy two would be to throw yourself in a screaming heap on the floor. If that didn't do it, you'd move up to the threatening to be sick routine, and so on. Fortunately, most adults have lost the determination to do whatever it takes, to learn from the lessons life throws at them, and have another go.

FORTUNATELY, most adults

have lost

the determination to do

whatever it takes,

to learn from the

lessons life

throws at them, and have

another go.

As Charles Handy said earlier, it's like learning to ride a bike. You have to take things one stage at a time. Move up one level at a time. Be prepared sometimes to take two steps forward and one back. When my son Tom was about four the magic moment arrived when he said, 'Dad, can you take the training wheels off my bike?' Well, it's a big job, what with the spanner and all, so I said, 'Are you sure Son, why now?' to which, like all four-year-olds, he replied: 'It's peer group pressure.' So I took them off and watched him go down the road, and do you know what? Crash! He fell off immediately. You know all about this, it's called being promoted to your level of incompetence. The thing is, you thought you'd already mastered it! Anyway, I encouraged him to get back on and after lots more trial and error (and a few cut knees) – success.

Action not to take

Don't keep track of your progress or how many attempts you've had. Instead protect your dignity by lying. If someone asks you, tell them you've had loads of goes at trying to achieve your goals. For example, in a suitably depressing tone of voice you could moan, 'I've tried hundreds of times to start a business.' This is a fantastic excuse, they won't even notice it's a ridiculous claim. I mean, it sounds so plausible. Even more so if you've also somehow convinced yourself it's true. Trust me, no one will think to check, so they'll never find out you really only tried once.

Step sixteen

Don't practise continuous improvement.

Quote to avoid

Here is Edward Bear, coming downstairs now, bump, bump, bump, on the back of his head, behind Christopher Robin. It is, as far as he knows, the only way of coming downstairs, but sometimes he feels that there really is another way, if only he could stop bumping for a moment and think of it.

Winnie the Pooh

Another way of describing what we've covered in the last few steps is Kaizen. Please have nothing to do with this funny Japanese word which roughly translates as 'continuous improvement'. The practice of Kaizen is responsible for the business revolution that took place in Japan after the war. Kaizen transformed the Japanese economy and made it the envy of the rest of the industrial world. Essentially it's a four-stage process:

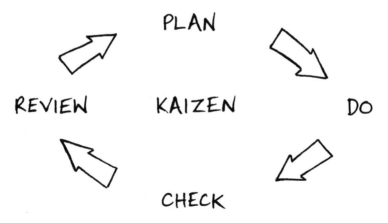

FIG 4 Continuous improvement

YOU

This is often about small, incremental improvements, evolution rather than revolution (successful individuals, and businesses, don't try to improve one thing by 1,000%, they try to improve 1,000 things by 1%). So, for example, if we were making a car:

➡ We come up with the plan or design.

➡ We make the car.

➡ As we make the car we consistently monitor that it's on the plan.

➡ After the car is finished we review and ask how it could be improved next time around. We then build these small, incremental improvements into our next plan and run through the cycle again.

The point is, where do failures spend most of their time? That's right, at stage 2, just doing stuff. Yet at what stage does all the improvement take place? Right again, at the end, when we review and build in the improvements for our next attempt. Few spend any time here but just rush off to get on with the next urgent thing. But, as the Japanese have proven, your long-term prosperity will be determined by how much time you spend working on your business compared with how much time you spend working in it. My advice is stay stuck at stage 2, in your hamster wheel, if you want to avoid all improvement.

Action not to take

Remember the quality of your life will be in direct proportion to the quality and depth of the questions you ask yourself on a regular basis. 'All of man's problems stem from his inability to sit quietly in a room,' said the philosopher Pascal. So don't do what Stephen Covey, the author of *Seven Habits of Highly Effective People*, suggests, which is to spend at least 30 minutes in review at the end of each and every day. If you do, don't ask focused questions like: 'What did I learn or relearn today, and how will it help me improve, even in just a small way, tomorrow?' Of course, if you did slip into this habit and your boss caught you sitting there at the end of the day, with your feet up on the desk and your hands behind your head, you'd have the perfect excuse. He asks you, 'What the devil do you think you are doing?' and you confidently reply, 'I'm continuously improving.'

Step seventeen
Don't wear a parachute.[1]

Quote to avoid

'Only those who will risk going too far can possibly find out how far one can go.'

T S Eliot

Key piece of advice. Don't do anything to upset the apple cart. Don't do anything different or new. Do zilch. Take no action. Zero. All failures know the easiest thing to do is to do nothing. However, if you do slip up, in terms of taking action, make sure that instead of small steps, you take gigantic leaps with the maximum chance of hurting yourself. Ignore the advice of William James who said: 'What should be preached is courage weighted with responsibility.' Instead be reckless and self-destructive and never mind the consequences. Never do any kind of risk analysis before you try anything new. Just leap, willy-nilly, out of aeroplanes without the aid of a parachute. This will be very messy upon landing.

In this way, as soon as you don't achieve the dizzy, significant heights you wanted (even though this is only your first time out), and rather than settle for average success, you can now easily justify giving up completely. 'After all,' you can moan to your family, friends and colleagues, 'I gave it my best shot at overnight success and look what happened. I crashed into the ground at 1,000 miles an hour and was dashed to a bloody pulp.' Adding, 'Never again' (emitting a deep sigh of resignation is also a nice finishing touch). Talking of Pulp, don't listen to Jarvis Cocker, their former lead singer, who said, echoing the sentiment of many other people before him: 'It's taken us 12 years to become an overnight success.'

[1] See Disclaimers at back of guide.

Organizing a massive cock-up, of your own making, every now and again, without, of course, taking any personal responsibility for it, is a great strategy. You're sure to put people off the scent that, in reality, you are a major coward with such little self-esteem it could easily be contained in a thimble.

ORGANIZING A massive cock-up, of your own making, every now and again, without, of course, taking any personal responsibility for it, is a great strategy.

If jumping out of planes, even with a parachute, seems too scary, use this as a convenient excuse not to jump out of planes at all. In fact, if you can convince people how dangerous doing anything new is, like changing jobs or starting a business, you won't even have to go to the airport.

Action not to take

Risk taking is a question of degree, like overtaking in a car – how far ahead do you have to be able to see before you are confident to overtake? 'If life is not a series of risks, then it is nothing,' said Helen Keller, who although profoundly blind and deaf, achieved so much in her life that she was voted one of the 20th century's top 100 people. Research says that people who have low levels of self-esteem generally plan their risks badly and typically produce terrible results. They have no memory bank of risk-taking episodes to build from and never fully analyze the consequences of their actions in advance. They make decisions slowly and change their minds quickly. Successful people do it the other way around. Failures usually quit after one attempt. To stay on the road, or should we say runway, to failure so should you.

Step eighteen
Don't change your beliefs.

Quote to avoid

' If I have the belief that I can do it, I shall surely acquire the capacity to do it even if I may not have it at the beginning. ' **Gandhi**

Think about it. Did you pop out of the womb with your beliefs already hard-wired in? No. So where do you get most, if not all, of your beliefs from when you are a child? That's right, your parents. Now, maybe you were unlucky enough to have parents who filled you with empowering beliefs about yourself and the world in general. A mum and dad who believed in you, who encouraged you to fulfil your potential, who taught you anything was possible, that you could be, do and have anything you deeply desired. Parents like that are rare. Which means the rest of us probably had parents who, in a well-intentioned attempt to avoid us being disappointed, or just to keep us safe, gave us a set of severely limiting beliefs. Just like the little boy who, in a really excited state, said to his dad, 'Dad, Dad, can I be an astronaut?' to which his dad replied: 'Don't be stupid, son, you come from Doncaster' (a place in England not known for its output of outer space adventurers).

So where do you think you get most of your beliefs from when you are a teenager? Yes, your peer group, other teenagers. Do you know any teenagers? Maybe you've even got some. Would you want their beliefs? Absolutely. A survey in the UK claims that by 14 years of age 98% of children have a negative self-image and feel insecure (what a marvellous start if you want to live a life of startling underachievement).

What I'm saying is, unless you've changed your beliefs – and by the way the most important beliefs are the ones you hold about yourself – you will definitely enjoy lasting failure.

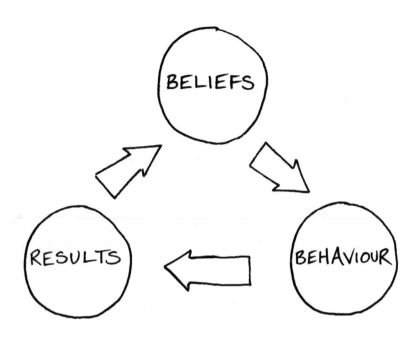

You see, many people reading this guide once believed in Father Christmas. Have you noticed how, when children believe in Father Christmas, it affects their behaviour? If they are misbehaving close to Christmas time, we parents only have to issue the threat 'he won't be coming' or 'all you'll be getting is coal' and our children immediately fall into line.

Beliefs are just things you feel certain about based on some references you've got. I think it was Tony Robbins who first described a belief as being a bit like a table. The table top was the belief and the legs of the table were what supported that belief. It's a great metaphor. Your parents told you Father Christmas existed, so there's one leg for your table. Your teachers did too, there's another. All your friends believed in him, that's a third leg. And on Christmas morning you got a fourth leg for your table when, magically, all these presents appeared. Yet at a certain age you managed totally to rearrange your entire belief system. Sometimes overnight you destroyed one table and built a new one just by changing your references. Firstly, some members of your peer group told you, 'Hey, it's your parents.' You confronted your mum and dad and they confessed. Your teachers owned up too. And now before Christmas it was a case of, 'Here's the toy catalogue, pick yourself a present.'

My son Finlay, when aged nine, confronted me with the big question: 'Does Father Christmas exist?' Parents be warned, this was in the middle of spring and completely out of the blue. So me and my wife told him, 'Well Finlay, you are a big boy now, so no he doesn't, it's just something parents made up.' Well, immediately the tears began to flow. And that was just me. Of course, we explained that our intentions in joining this worldwide conspiracy were honourable, but to not much avail. Then straight on the back of this, Finlay puts two and two together and, between gulps for air, looks me straight in the eye and asks: 'So how about the tooth fairies, they are real, aren't they?' 'Er, no,' I confess. Anyway, Finlay is tearful most of the night, and several hours later when I go to tuck him in bed he says: 'Dad, I've been thinking, no Father Christmas, no Tooth Fairy[1] . . . surely the Easter Bunny is real, isn't he?' More explaining, more tears. Here's the thing. Within moments Finlay had completely reconstructed his belief system and adjusted to a new reality. Next morning when

---

[1] The kid's tables (references) about tooth fairies were hard to shake. Myself and my wife had got into the habit of not only leaving money but also Post-it notes covered in tiny spidery writing that the kids thought were from a whole family of tooth fairies. We created a complete universe. My notes were always from Billy One Leg who had lost a leg to a cat but had had a wheel fitted so he could still dash around at high speed. Whereas the ones my wife wrote were from a posh fairy called Princess Crystal. My favourite from the princess was when she wrote (or was it my wife?), 'Dear Megan, I'm really cross because I have to do the night shift yet again because Billy One Leg is off sick with sticky wings.'

he got up, he was perfectly fine about it all. Now of course, I'm not suggesting that you could totally reconstruct your entire belief system in moments just like Finlay. I'm not saying it is easy to change your beliefs about anything just by changing your references. Or that by changing your beliefs you will immediately change your behaviour and therefore the results you enjoy.

The whole idea is that it has got nothing to do with what you believe to be true. It's got everything to do with how what you believe, usually at a deep, subconscious level, will determine how you behave, every minute of every day, for the rest of your life. And how you behave, on a consistent basis, will determine your results. Change the belief at one end and you change the results at the other. As Maxwell Maltz says: 'Within you right now is the power to do things you never dreamed possible. This power becomes available to you as soon as you change your beliefs.'

For when people believed the world was flat – and they once did – it didn't half limit travel. (Although you've got to admit Christopher Columbus wasn't exactly a master of goal setting – see step seven. Here was a man who set off and didn't know where he was going, when he got there he didn't know where he was, and when he returned he didn't know where he'd been.)

I remember when my daughter Megan was two and we suddenly realized that we were going on holiday in two weeks' time and she was still sleeping in a cot. My wife and I decided it would be great if she was used to sleeping in a bed. But we had only two weeks to train her to get used to the idea. When the two boys had swapped from cots to beds it had been a real struggle. Night after night we'd find them wandering about on the landing, screaming and bawling. In fact, we resorted to tying the bedroom door with string in an attempt to stop them escaping. Of course, cots are great because they are like little prisons, cell block 'H' and all that; the kids can't get out, you can dump them in and leave them to scream all night (just joking). So we thought, 'Let's just bite the bullet, we'll have to put up with the short-term inconvenience for the long-term gain.'

We carefully sold Megan on the idea of a bed. 'You're a big girl now and so you can have your very own bed,' we enthused. We get the new bed and the first night we tuck Megan in and she goes off to sleep sweet as a lamb. Then we sit downstairs waiting for the daring great escape and prepare ourselves for having to put her back into bed several times during the night. But guess what? We don't hear a peep all night. She doesn't get up once. We explain this away to ourselves as the fact that, of course, girls are much easier work than boys. Anyway, the next night it's the same routine. We tuck her in and not a peep all night. This goes on for a full seven nights. And then exactly a week after we started there is Megan screaming and bawling at four o'clock in the morning. And that's when I got it. Megan didn't realize you could get out of a bed. She had learned to be helpless; that because of her previous experience, nothing she did mattered, so why even try? (More on the fun of believing you are helpless can be found in step thirty.)

Another way we build beliefs is by generalizing from our experiences of the world. Have you noticed that just about everything is a generalization, including this sentence? This is a good thing when you are learning something new. Imagine if once you'd

HAVE YOU noticed that just about everything is a generalization, including this sentence?

learned how to open a door you had to figure out how to do it each time you approached one. No, having done it once, we generalize that this is how all doors work. However, generalizations can be a bad thing if you are trying to generate a different way of doing things. To prove it they once did an experiment where the hinges (which were hidden) and the door handle were on the same side of the door, like this:

HIDDEN
HINGES
ON SAME
SIDE AS
HANDLE

NEVER
THOUGHT
TO PUSH
DOOR HERE

Then they asked a load of adults to see whether they could open the door. Of course, they couldn't. They were stuck with their generalization for doors. The only explanation they could come up with for their failure was that they thought the door must be locked, which it wasn't.

I've met many women who have, with a good deal of venom, expressed the following view: 'All men are bastards.' Now typically, if you explore their experience, often they had a really bad time with one or possibly two blokes, who if truth be told were of uncertain parentage, but they then generalized it to be true of all of us fellas. Can you see if you construct a map of the world along these lines how difficult it would be to ever change your behaviour? Or get a decent boyfriend? By the way, in case you are wondering, all women are bitches too (obviously, I only said that to even up the score).

So please, please, please, if you want to remain a failure, don't mess with your beliefs.

Action not to take

Have you built a terrible table or a terrific table? We know a small percentage of people have radically different beliefs about themselves, life, work and everything to the vast majority of the population. These people know beliefs act as powerful filters to how you experience the world. They understand you don't believe what you see but rather you see what you believe. So if you believe that the world is a malevolent, bad place, it is. Or if you believe the world is a benevolent, good place, it is. The question is not which is true but which belief will serve you best in leading the life you want to lead. So please, don't ever compare your beliefs with those of these successful people (two of these master beliefs are discussed in the next two steps).

Step nineteen

Don't stop having a deep fear of failure and of making a fool of yourself.

Quote to avoid

'*Fear makes the wolf bigger than he is.*' **German proverb**

Are you scared? I should hope so. Many people I talk to are terrified. But what of? Well I know speaking in public is a biggie for many people. I think it's because we'd prefer anything to the humiliation of failure and making a fool of ourselves, especially in public. What is it with these professional speakers anyway? Are they crazy? Why would they want to put themselves in the position of looking an idiot on such a regular basis?

How they – and anyone else who steps outside their comfort zone – do it is by having a radically different belief to you. And here it is, get this, these people don't believe in failure. I know it's a bonkers belief, but there you are. Now, in the last few years I've managed to spend quite a bit of time with some of the most successful individuals and organizations on the planet (just so I could be certain of giving you the best advice on what to avoid doing). One of the curious things I've discovered is that they all believe the same thing: 'There is no failure, only feedback.' In fact, many have gone so far as to remove the word failure from their vocabulary (see step twenty-five). What does this belief actually mean? When you step outside your comfort zone you can only get one of two things. Either you succeed, which is highly unlikely if this is your first attempt, or more likely you fail. These successful folk say no, you only ever get one thing – results.

And as long as you have a way of feeding those results back into your next attempt, you can never fail. Take James Dyson, the inventor of the bagless vacuum cleaner. He first had the idea  in 1972 but you couldn't buy one in the UK until 1992. What do you think James Dyson was doing for those 20 years? I'll tell you: making cleaners that didn't work, learning from each attempt, until eventually he built one that did. So unlike Dyson, you mustn't stick at it. Even though another famous inventor, Thomas Edison, pointed out: 'Many of life's failures are people who did not realise how close they were to success when they gave up.'

All successful people have a deep-seated belief in themselves. Whatever happens – and you may have noticed in life and business 'stuff happens' (a sanitized version of a popular expression) – they never let it damage their self-belief. Neatly summed up by actress Sophia Loren when she said: 'Getting ahead in a difficult profession – singing, acting, writing, whatever – requires avid faith in yourself. You must be able to sustain yourself against staggering blows and unfair reversals. When I think back to those first couple of years in Rome, those endless rejections, without a glimmer of encouragement from anyone, all those failed screen tests, and yet I never let my desire slide away from me, my belief in myself and what I felt I could achieve.'

Action not to take

Forget that 'Why not!' is a slogan for an interesting life. Don't understand that if instead of aiming for perfect you were to focus on being outstanding, you would free yourself to be the best you could be. An idea best expressed by gold medal winner John Curry: 'The key for me in moving from being the British and

European champion to being World and Olympic champion at figure skating was giving myself permission to fall in competition.'

Don't adopt the belief that you can never, ever fail: all you can ever get are results.

Don't have robust feedback channels that can give you fast, accurate information on how you are doing. Don't listen to the advice of the founder of IBM, Tom Watson, who said: 'Fail fast and fail often.'

Leon Taylor won an Olympic silver medal in the 10-metre synchronized dive. I asked Leon when he first decided that he wanted to compete at the Olympics. Aged seven, he was watching TV with his dad when the man on screen stood on a podium. He was whistling the National Anthem. Leon asked his dad, 'Who is that, what is he stood on and why is he whistling?' to which he replied, 'Son, that is Daley Thompson. He's standing on a podium because he's just won an Olympic gold medal and the reason he's whistling is to stop himself from crying because he is so proud.' Leon decided he'd like to win one too and has used Daley Thompson as a role model ever since. That got me thinking about Daley Thompson, whose recipe for success comes down to the viewpoint: I'm good at this until proven otherwise. Approaching everything in the confident belief that you will excel is the polar opposite of the way most people face challenges. It's what Daley Thompson does, it's what Leon Taylor does, which is why if you want to fail you must never do it.

Step twenty

Don't take personal responsibility for your life and results.

Quote to avoid

'First, recognize that you are not a sheep who will be satisfied with only a few nibbles of dry grass or with following the herd as they wander aimlessly, bleating and whining, all of their days. Separate yourself now from the multitude of humanity so that you will be able to control your own destiny. Remember that what others think and say and do need never influence what you think and say and do.' **Og Mandino**

It's said that there are three types of people:

➡ those who make it happen;

➡ those who watch what happens;

➡ those who say, 'what happened?'

Naturally, if our goal[1] is developing lasting underachievement, then we want to ensure we belong to the third group. In order to do that, you must believe that where you find yourself today has little, if anything, to do with you. Everything – and I do mean everything, from what you do, how much you earn and who you are with – is a direct result of all the decisions you've made in your life, right up until this moment in time. And remember, a decision to do nothing is still a decision. You must continue to sit

---

[1] Obviously not a goal as such. You'll know from earlier in this guide, if you bothered to read it, which you probably didn't, that we certainly don't want clear, powerful, compelling goals.

back, make yourself totally unaccountable and irresponsible, and wait for someone else to show up, on possibly a white charger, bail you out and make things better. Mark Twain would encourage you not to do that by pointing out: 'Don't go around saying the world owes you a living; the world owes you nothing; it was here first.' But just put your hands over your ears until he goes away.

Some people argue that the key difference between humans and the rest of the animal kingdom is our conscious awareness. It's claimed we are the only species, apart from perhaps the odd dolphin, which has the freedom to choose our reaction to any given set of stimuli. We can just react or we can think before we react. The idea is that it's not what happens but how you respond to what happens that counts. You see, you might be pleased to hear that terrible things happen to successful people too. They just have a different response than you.

So just how response able are you? If you are like the average person you probably look for someone else or thing to blame. By the way, if you want an excuse for tolerating the blame culture that has grown up around us, you could blame it on the car insurance industry. Because what are you taught to do if you have an accident in your car? That's right, it's drilled into you: under no circumstances whatsoever admit liability. That's why accident insurance forms have included genuine comments like: 'As I approached the intersection, a stop sign appeared in a place where no stop sign had ever appeared before. I was unable to stop in time to avoid the accident' or 'An invisible car came out of nowhere, struck my vehicle and vanished.'

Now I'm not saying if you have an accident you should leap out of your car and cry 'it was all my fault', because it would probably affect your insurance, but I am saying successful people don't let this way of thinking permeate all the other areas of their life. One of the best bosses I ever worked for always took full responsibility for the results the team generated and never looked for excuses (even when we, the people who worked for him, knew there were plenty available).

So don't take ownership of your life, how you feel and the results you produce. Don't make your life all about getting results. Instead use a favourite of failures the world over – the 'wish' strategy. This is where you tell people you wish you could do something, for example: 'I wish I could drive.' This will fool people that, one day, you are actually going to take some personal responsibility and do something about it. Whereas you have no intention of ever trying. Or for the sake of variety, how about indulging in a burst of 'If only . . .' This is also a great expression for avoiding responsibility. For example, 'If only I'd had a better education . . . If only I had more money . . . If only my Dad wasn't an alcoholic . . . If only I didn't live here . . . If only I were younger . . . If only I were older . . . then I'd be much more successful.' (Need I go on? I'm sure you can think of loads of your own favourite excuses.) Don't, whatever you do, start to count how many times you wheel out these tired old excuses as a matter of habit, without even realizing that what you are truly expressing is just a series of limiting beliefs. Don't think that instead of wasting all that energy moaning you could be getting off your fat backside and doing something about it. Talk to any successful person and they'll all say in life there are only results or excuses. Which do you go actively looking for? You'll find some other choice excuses, posing as rational reasoning, to add to your repertoire in step twenty-six.

Do you feel you are a trapped victim of circumstance or a free creator of circumstance? At the end of every *Jerry Springer Show*, Jerry points out: 'No matter what your age, you are responsible for your own actions, irrespective of the actions or inactions of someone else. Past the age of legal reason, you and only you are accountable for what you do or don't do.' Yet if you look at the guests on the show, and the people in Jerry's audience, you'll see that being responsible for your actions and accountable for all your results is too hard a belief for most people to follow. It's much easier, for the vast majority, to blame things like circumstances, rather than themselves, for the fact that they've stood still for years or that things haven't changed for the better.

So would you feel at home on the *Springer* show? You certainly don't want to go on *Oprah Winfrey*, who points out: 'My philosophy is that not only are you responsible for your life, but doing the best at this moment puts you in the best place for the next moment.'

Action not to take

When Nikita Khrushchev, the Russian leader, was ousted from power, he sat down and wrote two letters and gave them to his successor. He said: 'When you get yourself into a situation you can't get out of, open the first letter and you'll be saved. And when you get yourself into another situation you can't get out of, open the second letter.' Anyway, soon enough this guy found himself in a tight place, so he opened the first letter, which said: 'Blame everything on me.' So he blamed the old man, and it worked like a charm. Well, he got himself into a second situation he couldn't get out of and he opened the second letter. It said: 'Sit down and write two letters.' The point is, you can only blame others for so long but it will at least buy you a bit of time before you have to stand up and be counted.

Don't ever say, 'I am 100% accountable and responsible for my life, for my feelings and for every result I get.' Don't put yourself at cause rather than at effect.

Don't listen to the advice of George Bernard Shaw, when he said: 'People are always blaming circumstances for what they are. I don't believe in circumstances. The people who get on in this world are the people who get up and look for the circumstances they want, and if they can't find them . . . make them . . .'

Step twenty-one
Don't stop believing in luck.

Quote to avoid

' Success is a matter of luck. If you want proof, ask any failure. ' **Earl Wilson**

Headingley in Leeds, England, is home to lots of artists, including my married friends Tom and Christine. Two things make this couple extremely rare, possibly even unique. Firstly, Tom and Chris paint on the same canvas, often at the same time, producing truly joint works of art (surprisingly they seem to be able to do this without any artistic or marital disputes).[1] Secondly, they are very, very lucky. Other painters in Headingley often say to them things like: 'I wish people would pay me what they pay you'; 'If only I had more time to paint, like you, instead of having to hold down a full-time job'; 'It's OK for you, I'd have to move to London to be as successful'; 'I can't ever imagine being as lucky as you with people ringing me up all the time, or knocking on my door, wanting to buy my paintings.'

I asked Tom about this. He says: 'Sure we're lucky. I mean OK, we used to have full-time jobs and could only paint at night. But because it's what we love to do, that wasn't a problem. We'd often stay up all night to get a painting finished. I always had a belief that we were good painters and that people would want to buy our stuff. I just started working my way through the phone book, calling hundreds of complete strangers, individuals, companies, restaurants, anybody I could think of, and seeing if they were interested in buying our paintings. It took me about two or three

[1] You can check out Tom and Chris's paintings at **www.reltonmarine.com**

years, and lots and lots of rejection, to learn how to sell our wares and get paid what we were worth. Eventually, we had enough work for me to concentrate on painting full time. Chris still held down a regular job, which helped pay the bills, whilst every spare moment she'd be painting or on the phone too, drumming up more commissions. At last, having built up a successful track record and after lots of searching, we found an agent and could now afford for us both to paint full time. Any of my friends could do what we've done, but first they'd have to stop using their favourite excuses like it's luck or if only this or if only that were to happen. They must stop waiting to be

DO YOU NEED MORE OF THESE?

discovered, for things to happen, and get off their backsides and do something about it. They must make it happen.'

Nice try Tom, but that's not going to stop us thinking you and Chris were just fortunate. You lucky people.

Don't be aware that when you change, commit to something new, you can expect resistance from everyone and especially your friends, or as William Penn Patrick puts it: 'No person, idea or institution becomes great until great resistance has been encountered.' Most people, unlike Tom and Chris, don't want to make waves or be criticized. Yet it's the criticism of friends and family that could be the biggest factor in holding you back.

Statistically speaking, if your parents didn't have children neither will you; five out of four people struggle with fractions; three out of four people make up 75% of the population; and 47.3% of statistics are made up on the spot. But what's certainly true is that the vast majority of people believe in luck. It's the best way to avoid responsibility. Trouble is, you can't take credit for the good stuff that happens either.

Action not to take

The thing I've noticed about Tom and Chris is that not only have they put in the hard work and the hours, but also they have not worried too much about how they would achieve all their goals. They just believed they would make it, then got busy doing anything they could. As a result, they've met all sorts of useful contacts, in unlikely places, and come across some amazing opportunities where you wouldn't expect to find them.

My daughter Megan, aged 11, came home from school the other day and said, 'Dad, do you believe in luck?' to which I replied, 'No but I do believe in synchronicity which means meaningful coincidences. That's where there is something you need and something turns up, apparently out of the blue, to help you. Tom and Chris use it all the time. Synchronicity, it's a beautiful word.' To which Megan said, 'I prefer the word solicitor or society.' Kids, they will mess with your mind!

I may believe in coincidences occurring to help you but I wouldn't rely on the heavens. But to be a failure you must. So don't stop looking at your horoscope every day. 'I don't believe in astrology. I'm a Sagittarian, and we're sceptical.' I think we can guess what Arthur C Clarke's view was about finding your fortune in the stars. You need to remain one of the thousands of people who look in the newspaper at their star sign to see if today will be their lucky day. Better still, call your horoscope hotline and at least you'll be making one person richer.

Don't examine whether people you think of as lucky really just did things you are scared of doing. Don't believe they took any kind of risks. Or were prepared to put up with years of rejection. Or were just ridiculously determined. Always put their success down to circumstances, accident, fluke and random chance.

Don't stop listening to the criticism of those, often closest to you, who don't like what you are doing and put any success you have down to good fortune (or being an Aries).

Step twenty-two
Don't expand your comfort zone.

Quote to avoid

'If at first you DO succeed, try something harder.' **Ann Landers**

Who are these strange people who actively seek out public humiliation and embarrassment? They are happy, and I do mean happy, to indulge in wanton experimentation and attempt new things in front of total strangers, or worse still, in front of family and friends. Amazingly, even when they know in advance that nine times out of ten they are going to fall flat on their stupid grinning faces, they still go ahead and do it. (Smiling, even though everything is going wrong, is a particularly annoying trait they all seem to share.)

And that's after we, as someone who cares for them, have given them the benefit of our vast storehouse of wisdom by telling them: 'Don't do it!' It's also a good idea at this point to go on and on, in graphic detail, about how ashamed they will feel when things, as they are bound to do, go pear-shaped. For good measure you could add: 'Listen, why should you be one of those people who wants the embarrassment of playing the violin in public and learning the instrument as you go along?' Even though they may, as one of your better educated friends, reply: 'Ah, as Jean Giraudoux said, "only the mediocre are always at their best",' Hopefully by now you've been negative enough to stop them dead in their tracks. Which is our goal. The last thing we want is for them to go off, try something, fail but be encouraged, try again and, after lots of trying, eventually succeed. Worse still, what if they succeeded first time out? How embarrassing would that be for us? Plus, if they start growing their comfort zone (terrible American phrase but there you are), it proves, if we shared their same beliefs, that we could too. And we don't want that. Even though you know that if your comfort zone isn't growing then it doesn't stay the same size, it actually shrinks. Just keep telling yourself and others: 'Mine's big enough, thanks.'

It's obvious that if you are going to be a real failure then it's really important to fear success. The fact is, if you do step outside your comfort zone (there it is again), you are going to have to become a different person. Someone with a new set of beliefs, knowledge and skills. As you start to enjoy success this will really start to annoy some of your friends. You will become a constant, irritating reminder that they could be achieving similar things to you if they weren't so scared. So they will drop you as a friend. That's why you should fear success. It will, God forbid, mean some of your friends will change. Then who would you have to sit around and go 'baaaa' with?

IT'S OBVIOUS that if you are going to be a real failure then it's really important to fear success.

Action not to take

Don't write in your 'to do' list, 'Step outside comfort zone today' – that way you'll forget to do it. Don't go and do the thing you fear the most, first. Don't step into the land of uncertainty at least twice a week. Don't do an uncomfortable thing until it becomes comfortable. Then, don't find the next uncomfortable thing and do that until it too becomes comfortable. And so on. Don't double the size of your comfort zone within the next 12 months, otherwise you'll become a massive success.

Step twenty-three
Don't use inside-out thinking.

Quote to avoid

Mind is the master power that moulds and makes, and man is mind, and ever more he takes the tool of thought, and shaping what he wills, brings forth a thousand joys, a thousand ills. He thinks in secret and it comes to pass; environment is but his looking-glass. **James Allen**

What's going to create a worse future for you is you. If you haven't already, wake up to the fact that the difference that makes the difference is you. Now you could carry on regardless, as you have been doing to date, giving no conscious thought to the world you are creating for yourself. But I think, if you want to be a spectacular failure, now is the time to think about what is going on, on the inside. Because it's what happens on the inside, not the outside, that counts. Now I know to date you've blamed everything in the outside world for you not getting what you want. This excuse works well because it's the one most people use. So don't be embarrassed to use it.

The following story illustrates my point. Two workmen sit down at lunchtime and open their lunch boxes. 'Oh no! Banana sandwiches again, what have you got, can I swap?' says the first workman to the second. 'No, I hate banana, especially in sandwiches,' comes the reply. Next day the same two workmen open their lunch boxes again. 'Oh no! Banana again, please swap.' 'Look,' says his colleague, 'I told you yesterday that I hate banana.' The third day exactly the same thing happens. 'Listen,' says the exasperated second workman, 'Why don't

Who made your sandwiches?

you get your wife to make you something different?' 'My wife?' says the first guy, 'I'm not married. I make my own sandwiches.'

You see, most of the things we complain about in life, we did. Life really is a do-it-yourself project and here's how to make a botched job of it. If you want to have a below-average job, a below-average relationship and a below-average life, just have below-average excitement, below-average dedication and below-average enthusiasm. The formula is simple: to have less, simply become less, from the inside out. Remember, work harder on other things than you do on yourself because only successful people do it the other way around. Console yourself with the thought that even if you stayed just the way you are, in our fast-changing world, you're still going to be left way, way behind.

Action not to take

If you are not happy about something in your outside world, put up with it. Never ask: 'What is it inside of me that causes this to happen?' Don't blame yourself for your lack of success. Don't believe that thoughts are causes and conditions are effects. Don't work on yourself first before you work on anything else.

Step twenty-four

Don't put things in before you try to take things out.

Quote to avoid

'They're only putting in a nickel, but they want a dollar song.' **Song title**

Ever tried cramming just hours before an important exam? Even in the unlikely event that you pass, within a matter of days, all the evidence proves, you'll hardly remember anything. This is just one example of what happens when you try to break the law. There are many ways of expressing this, the most powerful of universal laws. Here are just a few. 'Whatsoever a man sows, that also shall he reap.' Sir Isaac Newton called it the third principle of motion. He said: 'For every action there is an equal and opposite reaction.' Earl Nightingale put it like this: 'Your rewards in life are in direct proportion to your service.' And someone, nobody knows who, described this law as 'what goes around, comes around'.[1]

This law is the reason you have what you have right now. Which admittedly isn't much. Although you might not like it, the plain truth is that what goes out from you in any form must ultimately come back to you. It's just the way the universe works. By way of explanation, let's imagine if a farmer tried to cram like you did for your exams. What if, instead of planting his crops at the right time of year, then carefully cultivating and caring for them in the following months until harvest, he simply stuck them in the ground just before they were due for reaping? What kind of crop could he expect? Yet you think you can break this universal law and get things out without putting a blasted thing in.

[1] Probably Mark Twain again.

The best time to ignore this law is at the start of anything new. Get very impatient in the early stages of growth. You don't want to wait, you want it now, now, now, or even sooner than that. Go on, allow yourself to be depressed because the growth appears slow or non-existent. Don't remember that the farmer who plants his seeds must wait for them to take root. You don't see the farmer constantly digging up his seed to see whether it's sprouted, but you should constantly tear up your plans before they've been properly tested, charging off in the direction of yet another get-rich-quick scheme or overnight success (both of which you'll never find because, just like a free lunch, there is no such thing). And if you don't go looking for where the grass is greener, unlike the farmer, you must stand idly by and wait for things to happen. Whatever you do, don't tend the crop by watering and weeding. Don't nurture your crop in any way you can. Ignore Rudyard Kipling who said: 'Gardens are not made by singing "Oh, how beautiful," and sitting in the shade.'

GET VERY impatient in the early stages of growth. You don't want to wait, you want it now, now, now, or even sooner than that.

By the way, there is another universal law that sits alongside that of 'you only get out what you put in'. This law is based on the principle that nature abhors a vacuum. It states: 'If you want something better, first get rid of what you've already got.' Let me explain. At the back of our house is a paddock where the previous owners used to keep a horse. They hadn't had the horse for many years and had let the paddock become disused. The

NATURE DOESN'T LIKE THIS

whole area was overrun with weeds, nettles, thistles and grass up to your waist. I thought, one day, when I've got the time and the money, I'll turn that paddock into a fantastic playground for my kids. I'll get rid of all the weeds and have the whole thing turfed with beautiful green grass. Yet there it sat for nearly two wasted years while I waited to have enough money to change it.

Now not so long ago we found this great retired guy, called John, who once a week pops along and does a few jobs in the garden. I had happened to mention to John, in passing, my long-term vision for the paddock. Low and behold, I return home a few days later to find the whole paddock cleared. John had just gone ahead and done it. Well, they do say that the best people realize that, to get things done, it's always better to ask for forgiveness rather than permission. As I stood in the middle of the paddock it was amazing, now that everything had been cut down, how much easier it was to imagine what the finished thing would look like. Then it dawned on me that John had put the universal principle to work by 'making space'. Suddenly it seemed that it would be that much easier to complete the job because we'd first got rid of what we didn't want. Because we'd created a space I was much more motivated to fill it. Still, I've got to admit, I was concerned that it would be ages before I could get around to laying the grass. Then I bumped into John again. I thanked him for the work he'd done in the paddock. He told me that although I'd not asked him to do this either, he'd now measured up the land and got a quote for turfing the whole area. It was less than I thought but still too much. Then John says: 'Of course, if I was you, I'd only lay the turf a bit at a time between now and the summer. I could do that for you, it would be a lot cheaper and you'd only have to pay me a bit at a time.' What a brilliant solution. This new idea would never have occurred if first we hadn't rid ourselves of the old. Today the paddock looks great.

If you don't like those kitchen curtains, just sit there and put up with them. Don't take them down and give them away. Or don't go to your wardrobe and ruthlessly pull out everything you don't wear, or hate, and give them away. Remember, until you create space for the new it will never turn up. So not clearing things out will ensure that you get to continue to dress like a failure. (If you were, for some bizarre reason, to ignore my advice, a remarkable thing would happen. It wouldn't be long before your wardrobe was full of clothes again. The difference being it would be full of clothes you couldn't wait to wear.)

REMEMBER, until you create space for the new it will never turn up.

This principle also applies to your mind. You can't take in a new way of thinking about life, work and everything without letting go of your old way of thinking. To move on you must get rid of the clutter. So don't, whatever you do, cut down the weeds in your paddock.

Action not to take

Don't stop thinking you don't break the law. Don't even consider the fact that if you sit around doing nothing, all day and all night, you are still sowing nothing. Don't ever wonder what kind of harvest you can expect with that kind of sowing.

If you do till the soil, choose the seeds, wait for the right moment to plant and nurture the plants with care, don't expect the best from what you sow. Whatever you do, don't remember to walk away to let them grow. Forget you can't do the growing. You can only do what you know how to do and leave the garden to do what it does. Instead, stand over your goals every moment, anxiously willing them to happen, blocking out the sunlight they need. You'll wear yourself out and it will feel like hard work.

Don't make space for new things by first clearing out the unwanted things in your life.

Step twenty-five
Don't control your moods.

Quote to avoid

'I've suffered a great many catastrophes in my life. Most of them never happened.'

Will Rogers

For failures, their mood, or state, is determined by others or by their environment rather than by themselves. For instance, if someone says something negative about them, they feel terrible. Or if it rains they put themselves in a bad mood. You might say they get into a right state. Without giving it any conscious thought they bounce around from one state to the next hundreds of times a day. And in a typical day, many of those states prove to be extremely negative.

Now, if you think back to a specific time when you were in a less than resourceful frame of mind, what do you notice about your performance? No doubt it suffered. On the other hand, if you think about a similar situation when you performed at your absolute best, what was the key difference? You were the same person, with the same skills and knowledge, right? The difference was that you were in a better mood.

Your mood is determined by just the two Fs:

➡ **Fizzy**
Your physiology or everything that is physical about you (the way you move, breathe, stand, gesture, etc).

➡ **Focus**
Your mental focus (what you focus on in your mind, the sorts of questions you ask yourself, what you picture, feel and hear inside your head).

This is worth knowing because, what if, for no good reason, you suddenly found yourself in a good mood, performing at your peak, and were desperate to get back to your usual, low-perform-ance, grumpy self? Well, just change your Fizzy or Focus and you will instantly change your mood. Quickly sit with a physiology of acute depression, with your shoulders slumped, and ask yourself self-defeating questions in a whiny tone of voice. Such as: 'Why does this always happen to me?' Your brain will look for the exact answer and instantly tell you: 'Because you're a ninny!' By focus-ing on what you don't want rather than what you do want, you are doing an excellent job of confirming to yourself why you don't deserve something. This is guaranteed instantly to throw your state out of whack.

When you tell yourself something, you are sure to believe it, espe-cially on a subconscious level. Well, who would you believe, if not yourself?

Of course, if you're in a bad mood and would like to be in a good mood, I'm not suggesting that doing the exact opposite of the above would work.

Remember the original series of *Star Trek* with Spock and Kirk? I think it was the best. Typically an episode would begin with Cap-tain Kirk beaming down on to some planet or other with two new crew members, in red tops, whom we'd never seen before. Now I don't know about you but I'd be sat at home thinking, 'Well, you two are  dead, never to be seen in any future episodes.' However, Kirk would leave Mr Spock in charge on the bridge of the Enterprise. Suddenly they'd be attacked by the Klingons, and we all know how painful that is, and the crew would start running around like headless chickens, all, that is, except for Spock. He would be in what you might call 'The Spock State'. Do you remember his physiology? He'd be stood with his shoulders back and head up, totally centred, and relaxed. And it was always at this exact moment of crisis that Spock would use the 'F' word. Do you remember Spock's 'F' word? It wasn't Failure, it wasn't Feedback and it wasn't that other 'F' word that we are sometimes tempted to use in moments of stress when things appear to be going wrong. No Spock, whatever was going on, would calmly say 'Fascinating'.

Now this is one of the best state-changing words you can use, because the quickest way to change how you feel is to change your physiology and the quickest way to change your physiology is to put a big smile on your face.[1] For example, 'Hey Steve, you know that direct marketing campaign we ran, where we bought a list of 30,000 names, that cost us thousands of pounds, to send out an invitation to that big seminar you are running?' says one of my associates. 'Yes,' I reply. 'Well, I've just found out we've only received three bookings.' 'How fascinating,' say I. This causes me to crack a big smile. Which will in turn cause me to feel better. So don't you do it! (A further explanation of why you should avoid smiling can be found in step thirty-four.) Not only will saying 'Fascinating' impact on your physiology, it will also change your focus. You see, I think all Spock was doing was asking a much better question. I think he was saying, 'Listen, can we all stop running around like headless chickens for one moment and look at this result because I think there is something fascinating to learn here. But if you stay all

---

[1] One technique lots of salespeople use is this. Next time you are going for, say, an important meeting, and you are not feeling great, just before you go in put a big stupid grin on your face. You will have to 'fake it till you make it' but what happens is your mind and body goes 'Hang on a minute, he's got a smile on his face, he must be happy' and then the feeling will quickly follow. However, be careful not to over do it because as comedian George Carlin observes: 'If a man smiles all the time, he's probably selling something that doesn't work.'

upset, take it personally and beat yourself up, then we could miss what there is to learn, stay feeling bad and not be able to build the learning into our next attempt.' He was of course also demonstrating childlike curiosity at the stuff life – and in his case the universe – threw his way.

Abraham Maslow, a motivational expert who for years studied why people behave the way they do, said people who had self-actualized (why he couldn't just have said happy people is beyond me) displayed the following characteristics. They had learned to become independent of the good opinion of other people. They had no investment in power over people. They had no interest in trying to convince anybody else or dominate anybody else with their opinions or abilities. And they didn't mind disapproval – to them it was like water off a duck's back. Without causing offence to anyone, they simply didn't let what folk thought determine how they should feel. Nor did they let it get in the way of their dreams, goals and ambitions. However, dear reader, don't you stop sucking up to and trying to please everyone in order to feel good.

DEAR READER, don't you
stop sucking up to
and trying to please
everyone in order to
feel good.

Action not to take

As I've said already, what's really going to damage your chances of failure is if you start acting like a kid again. Nor must you ever catch yourself saying 'How fascinating' the next time a calamity befalls you.

Remember that another easy way to control your moods is to control your focus by asking yourself better questions. 'What can I find that is good in this situation?' 'What have I learned from this that will make me more successful the next time?' 'How can I make this situation better?' If you were to ask yourself better questions like these you would force your brain to look for choices and find solutions. Instead, don't stop asking yourself self-defeating questions like: 'Why am I so scared?' 'What did I do to deserve this?' and 'Why does nobody like me?' Because quick as a flash your brain will fire back the exact answer. As it says in the Bible: 'Ask and you will receive.' What is it you want to receive? Good news or bad news? Don't regularly ask yourself, 'Am I enjoying this thought?' And if you do ask the question, and you don't like the thought, don't realize you have the power to change it instantly. After all, you can hold only one thought in your head at a time. Do you really mind if it's a good or a bad one?

Don't think about how you can instantly change what's going on in your body, or your mind, in order to change how you feel. Continue to blame the weather. Or other people. Or even getting out of the wrong side of the bed in the morning.

Step twenty-six
Don't transform your language.

Quote to avoid

'Handle them carefully, for words have more power than atom bombs.'

Pearl Strachan

I've got a question for you: 'So you talk to yourself?' You know that little voice inside your head. Can you imagine if you talked out loud to your family and friends how you talk to yourself, do you think you'd have any? Of the thousands of things you say to yourself every day, inside your head, how many are positive and how many are about what a lousy screw-up you are? You may be surprised to learn that something as simple as the voice inside your head could be the one thing that will determine whether you're a success or failure in life, work and everything. But it's true. Now unless you are possessed, spinning head, green vomit, that kind of thing, then did you know it's your voice? Now because it's you, talking to yourself, you can consciously choose, in an instant, what you are going to say. I once told someone this and they said: 'Don't be stupid, it talks and you have to listen.' Which is an excellent belief to have if you want to continue listening to negative self-talk for the rest of your life (and who wouldn't?).

Are you also whining your way to alienation out loud? Please don't stop telling as many people as possible how terrible and incapable you are at so many things. Why should you, they love doing it too. This is what I call low self-esteem ping-pong (table tennis to our more upmarket readers). To play, first serve with something like: 'Guess what, they've asked me to do a presentation to the board . . .' Significant pause. '. . . And I'm the worst presenter in the world.' To which whoever you are talking to replies: 'If you think you're useless at presentations, you should see me, I'm even worse than you.' You counter with: 'Mind you, if you think my presentations are bad, you should see my timekeeping.' The game continues until you have proven you are lousy at more things than the other person. Remember, if you argue for your own limitations, they are yours to own.

Of course, when we say this kind of stuff out loud what we are looking for are a few sympathetic strokes back and the odd 'there, there, poor thing'. Perhaps what you don't realize is, although we may feel we're telling other people this stuff, who is actually hearing this rubbish the most? You are, because your mouth is nearer your ear. You are reinforcing a self-fulfilling prophecy. Isn't it good to know that your most reliable ally in the quest for failure is yourself?

Action not to take

Don't make yourself accountable for your own internal and external dialogue. Just let it gabble on like a runaway train. A huge percentage of emotions come from how you talk to yourself. So don't regularly monitor what you say inside your head. Don't adopt this guideline: that you promise never to say anything inside your head, to yourself, that if someone came up and said the same thing to your face you'd be mortally offended. And also don't keep careful tabs on how often you say out loud to others how useless you are. Don't stop saying things like 'I can't' when really what you mean is 'I won't'. Don't replace 'I'll try' with 'I choose not to'. Disregard Yoda who, in *The Empire Strikes Back*, tells Skywalker: 'Either do or do not. There is no try.' That's great coming from a puppet with a hand stuffed up his . . .

Step twenty-seven
Don't think about the first four minutes.

Quote to avoid

'I was so ugly when I was born, the doctor slapped my mother.'

Henry Youngman

First impressions are important, aren't they? I was going to put this quote at the top of the page: 'A smile increases your face value' – but thought if it makes me want to throw up it might have the same effect on you.

In just a moment I'm going to share with you perhaps the most powerful idea in this book. It's the one idea, which I've been sharing on stage with thousands of people all around the world for the past 15 years, that I get the most positive feedback on in terms of improving your relationships with family, friends, customers and prospects. So it is really important if you want to create bad impressions that you skip the next bit.

For example, in research done with juries after a trial, and with mock juries in experiments, when asked the question, 'When did you decide the defendant was either guilty or innocent?' it's been discovered the answer was within four minutes. There is some evidence to say it could even take as little as seven to seventeen seconds of interaction with strangers before they form an opinion of us (then you've got up to four minutes to recover from a negative impression before it becomes lasting). In other words, most people take one look at the defendant, before they've even had a chance to open their mouth, and decide either guilty or innocent. Then the filters go up and all they hear for the rest of the trial is anything that proved them right in the first place.

This is why, allegedly, O J Simpson employed eight image consultants for his trial (I don't know if one of them was Mr Pink from step forty-one).

In another experiment, featured in a TV programme about the human mind presented by Professor Robert Winston, six men dressed identically in black, including black woolly hats. They were put one at a time in front of a mock jury of 12 people who were then asked, based on appearance alone, who looked most guilty. The results were that the jury felt that people with symmetrical faces, or if you like reasonably good looking people, were less guilty. Whereas people with asymmetrical faces, or in other words ugly people (and you know who you are), were felt overall to be more guilty looking. You may cry, 'Not fair!' but that's just how it is. Clichés are often true, that's why they are clichés. So although film mogul Samuel Goldwyn said, 'Avoid clichés like the plague,' I for one will ignore him because it turns out you really never do get a second chance to make a first impression. This means if you're unlucky enough to have a face that looks like a bulldog chewing a wasp, you're going to have to work twice as hard in those first four crucial minutes. Although I love Jean Kerr's comment: 'I'm tired of all this nonsense about beauty

IT TURNS OUT you really never do get a second chance to make a first impression.

being only skin deep. That's enough. What do you want – an adorable pancreas?'

Of course, the four minute rule really comes into its own when applied to customer care (although I feel customers as a minimum expect to be cared for, so maybe we should think more in terms of customer experience). Getting it wrong is, let's say, when you come to check in at a hotel. It's late at night, you've had a tiring journey, and to cap it all as you cross from the car park to the hotel the heavens open, it pours with rain and you get soaking wet. Now you find yourself standing in a damp puddle at the reception desk, cold, wet and miserable, and you just want to get to your room and enjoy a warm bath. BUT there's no one behind reception to check you in. Now, if the hotel does this kind of thing to you, the research says, and your own personal experience will back this up, that even if you were to stay at that hotel for two weeks and the rest of the time it was OK, the bit you remember – the bit you tell your friends and colleagues about (and sometimes because you are so hacked off, complete strangers) – is the first four minutes.

Some hotels have so locked on to the importance of this that they've completely re-engineered the first four minutes. They've fired the doorman, they've fired the receptionist, they've fired the person who carries your bag and instead made them all just one person called a greeter. Now when you show up, a smartly dressed individual, possibly wearing more expensive clothes than you asks: 'Excuse me Sir are you checking into the hotel?' 'Yes,' you say, to which they reply: 'Welcome to the hotel, my name is Chris and I'm here to greet you. Could I just take your name please?' 'Er yes, it's Steve McDermott.' (Tip: only say this if you are me or it is in fact your name.) The greeter then looks up your details in a little electronic keypad they are carrying and says: 'Follow me Mr McDermott, I will check you into your room.' You think they are going to take you to reception. No, they take you straight to your room. The goal is to get you settled in as soon as possible. Wow! A bit different from the damp puddle experience, isn't it?

I got thinking about this and, many years ago, began an experiment with my most important customers just to see if the four minute rule was really as important as it would appear. Now I don't know about you, but my most important customers were at one time quite small (I mean height wise) and quite demanding. I'm of course talking about my kids. When they were little, if I was ever away overnight on business, or especially away several nights, then typically on my return this would happen. I arrive home grubby and tired from travelling, I've been on a plane and then in a car for hours. I open the front door and am greeted by three small bodies hurling themselves at maximum velocity down the hall and attaching themselves limpet-like to my arms and legs whilst shouting in unison at the tops of their squeaky voices, 'DaaaaaaaD!' Now in the past, right at that moment, it had been really tempting to say, 'Kids, will you just let me get in the house, take off my coat, put my bag down.' However, understanding the four minute rule I don't do that any more, but I did have to train myself. I did this by first putting a Post-it note on the dash of the car which said 'check your mood' (otherwise I was liable to forget), then when I was about a couple of miles from home I'd check my mood. Well, if I was in the car I might have been driving for a while and might be a bit crumpled. The fastest way to change how you feel you'll remember, going back to the two 'Fs' in step twenty-five, is firstly to change your physiology. So I might sit up straight, look in the rear view mirror and put a big stupid grin on my face, and to help I might whack on a favourite piece of music, one I've especially saved just for this moment.[1]

---

[1] My choice is a truly brilliant piece of Northern Soul (see back of guide), 'Better Use Your Head' by Little Anthony & The Imperials.

Then, also to change my mood, I'd change my focus by asking a high quality question. It's a question that you can adapt to almost any situation. My question is, 'How would the best dad in the world act when he walked in that door?' and that's how I act. Now here's the really good news. You only have to keep it up for FOUR MINUTES, because that's the bit they remember. Here's the even better news. Once you've bothered to get in a better mood, and let's be honest it's not much effort, and you find yourself rolling about on the carpet with the kids, it's quite pleasant – and the more you do it the easier it becomes. So you've created this virtuous circle, until before you know it, you're managing all these little four minute interactions throughout the day, most times without even consciously thinking about it.

Action not to take

Don't put your focus on the first four minutes. The top hotels, top organizations and top people have re-engineered the first four minutes of every interaction to make it a massively positive experience for the person on the receiving end. Sometimes it will be a simple step, like how you sign in at reception when you visit their offices. Here are some experiences I have had:

➡ Fill in a form yourself which the receptionist then puts in a badge for you to wear. She does this after she has interrogated you about the purpose of your visit. A little bit like when you check in at an hotel and they ask for your credit card in such a manner it sounds like they are saying, '...we need this because I can tell you are a thieving Northern bastard who is gong to steal all the furniture'.

➡ Fill in the form yourself, but this time typing all your details including car registration into a computer screen which then prints out a badge for you to wear (very perplexing when you're at the front of a long queue of sales reps and, because they are watching, you now can't even remember how to type your own name).

➡ You arrive at your destination and a sign says, 'This car parking space reserved for Steve McDermott.' At reception another sign says, 'ABC Ltd welcomes Steve McDermott.' Before you have chance to speak the receptionist says, 'You must be Mr McDermott, welcome, here is your badge' (which had been printed before your arrival).

Any guesses which experience I prefer? You see, most systems are set up to suit the organization, whereas they should be re-engineered to suit the customer.

Step twenty-eight
Don't talk and think about what you want.

Quote to avoid

'Man invented language to satisfy his deep need to complain.'

Lily Tomlin

IF THIS WAS IN COLOUR, DON'T THINK IT WOULD BE BLUE.

Do you know it's totally impossible to process a negative in your neurology? For example, just stop for a moment – now I don't want you to think of a blue elephant. What are you thinking of? That's right, a blue elephant. Yet we do this kind of thing all the time. I remember when my daughter Megan was about two-and-a-half years old – this was a mere six months after she'd learned that a bed wasn't a prison[1] – and she came into the living room carrying a large glass of milk. There had been no spillage problems so far, but as a clever grown-up I could see it happening. So I say, 'Hey Megan, don't drop that milk.' With a big smile on her face Megan drops the milk and there's an almighty smash. When this happens I immediately shout, what all parents shout in these circumstances: *'What did I say?'* To which Megan replies, the way

---

[1] Beds not being prisons will make no sense if you were naughty and skipped step eighteen.

any two-and-a-half-year-old would: 'Well, Dad, you're always going on about the fact you can't process a negative in your neurology. What you actually said was "Drop the milk, don't," you see I can't think about not dropping the milk without thinking about dropping it.' Just for good measure she also added: 'It's a bit like some of your other all-time favourites, "Don't play in the road, don't bite your nails, don't wet the bed and don't talk to strangers." Can you see now why I do all of those things?' She's right.

The fact is, you become what you think and talk about most of the time. Now, strictly speaking, if that were true, most adolescent boys would, in point of fact, be adolescent girls, but you get the idea. The point is, successful people only think and talk about what they want most of the time. And what do failures talk and think about most of the time? That's right, what they don't want. People in sales are often guilty of this. I've many times overheard a salesperson, on the phone, say: 'I don't want you to think I'm giving you some kind of a hard sell.' Now, up until this point, you could tell the conversation was going rather well. It took the salesperson to put their foot in their big fat mouth.

SUCCESSFUL people

only think and talk about what they want most of the time.

Businesses in general are just the same. I was in a hotel bathroom the other night when I noticed a small sign under the towel rail. It said: 'Do not steal our towels. We will charge you £5 per towel.' Well, I got one of the large bath towels and held it up. It must have been five feet long and was very thick and fluffy. I thought, this has got to cost at least £25 in Marks & Spencer. So I stole five. But I've got to tell you it never occurred to me until they told me not to. So for maximum disruption, accidents and loss, make sure all your business communication from safety signs to company memos tell people what not to do – that way you'll know they'll go right ahead and do it. It beats me why computer companies put in big bold writing: 'Don't make copies of this disk.'

Action not to take

You become what you think about. You become what you focus on. That's why your entire life, right up until this moment, is a reflection of the quality of questions you ask yourself. Remember all unimprovement is a result of asking terrible questions. Questions centred around what you don't want to happen ensure that's what will happen. So, don't start thinking, and talking, about what you do want for yourself and others. Because I don't want you to think this is not easy to slip into right now.

Step twenty-nine
Don't go to the movies.

Quote to avoid

'Formulate and indelibly stamp on your mind a mental picture of yourself as succeeding. Hold this picture tenaciously. Never permit it to fade – and your mind will seek to develop the picture.' **Norman Vincent Peale**

Here is a bizarre and little-known fact. Your brain and body can't tell the difference between something you vividly imagine and reality. Truly. Almost all world-class sportsmen and women are visualizers. As are other peak performers in just about any other field you care to mention. All these people see it, they feel it, and they experience it, before they actually do it. As a formula this would be: $I \times V = R$ (Imagination $\times$ Vividness = Reality). The secret is the symbol in the middle, repetition. Repetition – that's repetition – it would seem really is the mother of all skills.

Of course, apart from positive visualization there is another name for this. It's called worry. What failures do is vividly imagine things going terribly wrong in full Technicolor with quadraphonic sound, over and over and over again. They don't understand that fear is that little darkroom where negatives are developed. The point is, in life you always get what you focus on. So don't be aware that it is actually entirely up to you whether you use this special gift to generate good or bad results. Now maybe you are thinking, surely what I think about can't allow me to do something I've never done before or create physical results. Well, yes it can. You see, by constant repetition you coat the neural pathways in the brain. This effectively creates fake but totally believable memories. Specialists in brain research give the following explanation: 'When you learn anything, a pattern of neurons is set up in your brain tissue. The chain, or electrical pattern, is your brain's method of remembering, so since the subconscious cannot distinguish a real from an imagined experience, perfect mental practice can create new patterns or correct imperfect patterns grooved here.'

Visualization has a definite effect on the body's electroencephalographic waves. (EEG waves are a measure of electrical activity in the brain.) If you imagine yourself running, small but measurable contractions actually occur in the muscles of your body.

Now it may sound like a couch potato's dream, but recent research has proven you can even think yourself strong with imaginary exercises. Researchers asked ten volunteers aged 20 to 35 to imagine flexing one of their biceps as hard as possible in training sessions five times a week. The researchers, whose findings were reported in the magazine *New Scientist*, recorded the electrical brain activity during the sessions. To make sure volunteers were not unintentionally tensing and moving their arms, they also monitored electrical impulses of their arm muscles. Every two weeks muscle strength was measured. The volunteers who thought about exercise showed a 13.5% increase and maintained that gain for three months after the training stopped. Or how about this – psychologists have developed a mental training system that improved the golf putting skills of volunteers by more than 50% after only six weeks. The player must practise in his head for ten minutes a day while watching a video of himself playing, or while listening to an audio tape of his putts being holed. He can stand in his living room holding a club, or simply recreate the movements in his head whilst sitting. Men who used the video method improved by 57%. Those who listened to a tape improved by 47%. One group improved by 18% after simply reading a biography of Jack Nicklaus[1] for ten minutes a day. Dr Smith of Chester College and Dr Paul Holmes of Manchester University are responsible for the study. Says Dr Smith: 'Nicklaus always said he imagined where the shot would go – and then it would go there.' Dr Holmes says: 'The technique works by strengthening the mental pathways involved in making a putt. It's like walking through a cornfield. There is a faint pathway the first time you do it, but the more you tread along the same path, the stronger it gets.'

One of the greatest exponents of running mind movies, who coincidentally was known as The Greatest, was Muhammad Ali, the former World Heavyweight Boxing champion. Ali called it 'future history'. Ali said: 'The man with no imagination has no wings.' He always rehearsed the fight in his head, over and over, before he ever stepped into the ring. That's one of the reasons why out of the 19 fights in which he predicted the outcome (when he'd say things like 'Archie More, you're going in round four'), 17 happened exactly the way Ali said they would. With Ali winning. What people say is, if this technique is so powerful, what about the fights that Ali lost? His answer was that his opponents had just created a stronger future history than him. But I ask you, with only 17 out of 19 correct predictions, is it really worth bothering with even a few minutes of mental rehearsal? Even though five times Olympic gold medallist Sir Steve Redgrave personally told me: 'Steve I probably spent more time training in my head than I ever did sat in a boat!' Doh! What does he know about success?

---

[1] Remember back at step eleven I suggested you don't read lots of biographies because it's bound to improve you. Now it seems that even includes your golf game.

By the way, if you think all you have to do is imagine success and it's then served up on a plate, I've got news for you. For Ali also said: 'The fight is won or lost far away from witnesses. It is won behind the lines, in the gym and out there on the road, long before I dance under those lights.' Ali was talking about the accumulative effect of training in your head and your body. He thought that to be in the real top flight you had to do hours and hours of hard physical work, as well as disciplined mental rehearsal. Oh dear!

Action not to take

Thoughts are things, so don't run your own mind movies. If you do, don't focus on what you want. Please be very careful what you think about because this powerful technique works for both positive and negative things. Imagine if I set you the following exercise. For the next 30 days, every morning when you wake up and swing your legs out of bed, just for 60 seconds I want you vividly to imagine getting really ill. How do you think you would be feeling after a month?

That's right, not great. Now what if instead every morning when you woke up and swung your legs out of bed and this time just for 60 seconds you were vividly to imagine having a great day and feeling full of energy and glowing health. After 30 days how would you be feeling? So don't, whatever you do, start vividly imagining yourself as a success.

Forget that the key ingredient to success isn't knowledge but the power of your imagination. Or as Emile Coue, author of *Self Mastery Through Conscious Autosuggestion* – a mouthful of a title which simply means saying daily affirmations to yourself in order to, for example, bolster your confidence – put it: 'When will comes into conflict with imagination, the imagination always carries the day.'

FORGET THAT the key

ingredient to success isn't knowledge but the power of your imagination.

And if you do fall into the habit of imagining your future success, don't do any of the physical work involved in increasing your knowledge or developing a new skill that goes with it.

Step thirty

Don't stop being an unthinking dog.

Quote to avoid

'If dogs could talk, it would take a lot of the fun out of owning one.'

Andrew A Rooney

Don't scientists make you laugh? Take Ivan Pavlov. I mean, how do you wake up one morning and think', 'I know what I'll do today, I'll get some dogs (he just so happened to have some about the place) and see if I can build a stimulus and response mechanism in their neurology outside of their conscious awareness'? Pavlov got a hungry dog and gave it some meat, and at the exact moment he gave it the meat, he rang a bell. He only had to do this on average five times to establish a stimulus and response mechanism. To test this he didn't offer the dog any meat but just rang the bell and the dog still watered at the mouth. What he discovered is that dogs have ears (thanks to Eddie Izzard for that gag). No, seriously, he proved the bell now had a new meaning or association for the dog.

'Steve, what's this got to do with anything?' I hear you ask. Well, we are dogs too. If you are in a long-term relationship, you'll have a mass of associations, most of which are negative, all of which will have been built up, over time, outside of your conscious awareness. Take music. If you are married there is probably one piece of music you strongly associate with your wedding (remember you and your beloved having the first dance to, let's say, 'You are the wind beneath my wings' – aaaah!). Now, years later, you are driving along when suddenly 'your song'[1]

---

[1] I only have to hear another Northern Soul classic (see back of guide), 'It really does hurt me girl' by The Carstairs, one of my other all-time favourite records, and I'm catapulted through time on to the dance floor of The Highland Room, Blackpool Mecca, circa 1973.

comes on the radio. Instantly, without even thinking about it, you will feel a certain way, especially if you are now divorced. Smell is another powerful anchor to which many of us have a conditioned response. I remember being in a restaurant with my wife Candy. She smelt some really fresh olive oil and was instantly transported back to the kibbutz in Israel where she'd spent six months working (I'm still waiting for her to come home).

Those wacky people in advertising know all about building conditioned responses in us gullible consumers. For instance, complete the following: 'A Mars a day helps you work, rest and . . .' or 'Mild green Fairy . . .'. The answers are of course 'play' and 'Liquid' (by the way, for our American friends, Fairy Liquid is only for doing the washing up). **WHO IS RINGING YOUR BELL ?**

The point is, a peak performer deliberately uses conditioned responses to put themselves into a resourceful state. Why do tennis players constantly twiddle their racket round and round in their hand just before receiving a serve? Because it puts them in the right state. Still, tennis isn't a proper game, so who cares?

Dogs have also helped prove the existence of something called learned helplessness. Now, out of all the beliefs you can have, this is without doubt the most destructive and damaging. In fact, the study and understanding of learned helplessness is recognized as one of the most important psychological breakthroughs of the last 100 years. A key experiment that first established this learned behaviour took place in the 1960s and was conducted by Dr Martin Seligman of the University of Pennsylvania. Dr Seligman had noticed that while testing some dogs – by giving them electric shocks – some didn't respond but just lay down, whimpered and stayed in pain. (Before our animal-loving readers go ballistic, Dr Seligman's explanation for carrying out these types of experiments was that he believed he could find a cure for depression.)

Seligman devised a clever two-stage experiment to discover why some dogs simply gave up. In stage one, dogs in Group A were given a mild electric shock. The dog could stop the shock by pressing a bar with its nose. It soon learned to do this. Dogs in Group B were also given the same electric shock but had no way of switching it off. Dogs in Group C were given no shocks.

The next day, stage two of the experiment took place. The dogs were placed, one at a time, in what Seligman calls a shuttle box. This is a box with a low barrier down the middle. One side of the box is electrified, the other isn't. The dogs were put on the side where they would receive a continuous, mild electric shock. To get away from the pain, all the dogs had to do was to jump the low barrier to get to the other side. Here is what happened. Group A dogs (those that could control the shocks) and Group C dogs (those which had been given no shock) almost immediately learned they could jump the barrier to get away from the pain. But the Group B dogs (those that could not control the shock in stage one) didn't even try to escape. They simply lay down and whimpered.

What Dr Seligman, and many others since, had discovered is that these dogs had lost their motivation to act. Now as I've said, we are dogs too. In fact, we are worse. Guess how many times it takes a human to learn to be helpless? In one experiment a group of volunteers were placed in a room with several doors leading from it. All the doors were locked and then a very loud noise was pumped into the room. The volunteers immediately tried to get out of the room, but upon discovering that all the doors were locked, simply sat back down and put up with the appalling din. Unbeknown to them, straight after they had tried the doors, the scientists had very quietly unlocked them. The thing is, not one volunteer got up and tried the doors again. They had learned to be helpless in just one go. Like lots of folk, they had the belief that what they did didn't matter, so why bother? It's my observation that many organizations are suffering from learned helplessness. This undermines all their attempts to motivate people or introduce effective change.

If you've already learned to be helpless, the worst thing you can do is become aware of it, as this would encourage you to have another try. To ensure you don't fall into this trap it's worth understanding something that evolves from learned helplessness, and that is that your success, or for that matter failure, in life will be largely determined by the way you explain or respond to life's events. Dr Seligman calls this your explanatory style. Here are two crucial elements to your explanatory style.

Permanence

People who fail and give up easily believe that the causes of the bad events that happen to them are permanent. They can't see past their current circumstances. Whereas achievers, happy people, when they meet problems rarely see them as permanent. They believe the causes of bad events are temporary. Their motto is, 'All things must pass.'

ACHIEVERS, happy people, when they meet problems rarely see them as permanent.

Helplessness can also result from letting the problem spread. Whilst a problem might be a big one, optimists will not let it affect the rest of their lives. They put a ring fence around the problem and contain it. As Dr Seligman says: 'Some people can put their troubles neatly into a box and go about their lives even if one important aspect of it – their job, for example, or their love life – is suffering. Others bleed all over everything. They catastrophize. When one thread of their lives snaps, the whole fabric unravels. It comes down to this: people who make universal explanations for their failures give up on everything when failure strikes in one area. People who make specific explanations may become helpless in that one part of their lives yet march stalwartly on in others.'

Action not to take

Don't deliberately think about what triggers bad moods in you. Don't think about what could trigger good moods in you, like a favourite piece of music, picture or memory. Don't create a gap between the stimulus and response (like counting to ten) before you decide how to feel or react.

Don't have another go at something you've tried loads of times before and gave in believing you could never succeed. You may find that, today, you can do it. If you explain failure as permanent (nothing will ever change) and pervasive (all bosses are unfair), you will forever be locked into pessimism. If you explain failure as temporary (there is always tomorrow) and limited (the boss is in a bad mood today), you will forever be an optimist. Which is it you want to be? Great big silly, salivating dog that you are.

Step thirty-one

Don't ask, 'How do you do that?'
Don't act 'as if'. And don't be naïve.

Quote to avoid

‘I pretended to be somebody I wanted to be, until I finally became that person. Or he became me.’ **Cary Grant (formerly Archie Leech)**

If you've never done something before, don't find someone who has, and don't ask them the question: 'How do you do that?' And never add: 'Oh, and can I take notes?' Having asked that question of loads of successful people, on planes, trains and automobiles, and anywhere else I come into contact with them, again purely for research, do you know what happens? Sometimes they tell me, in just ten minutes, something it took them 25 years to find out. You must never do the same.

I once asked Richard Emmanuel, a young Scottish entrepreneur, who at the time had just sold part of his mobile phone empire for several million pounds, 'How did you do that?' He just smiled and said: 'I did what you just did.' He went on to explain that he had started his business a few years before with one mobile phone retail outlet in Scotland. However, he did have the belief and vision that he could grow it into a chain of outlets throughout Scotland and eventually the whole of the UK, he just wasn't sure how. So one day he thought, 'Who do I know who has already grown a successful chain of retail outlets in Scotland and the rest of the UK?' Because he'd asked such a great, focused question, quick as a flash a name popped into his head: Sir Tom Farmer. Now in case you don't know, Tom Farmer is also a Scot and the man behind the highly successful nation-wide chain of Kwik-Fit tyre and exhaust centres. Richard got hold of Tom's phone number and decided to give him a call.

Now at this point you may be thinking, hang on a moment, surely a busy, successful person, especially if he is a sir, isn't going to take a call from a complete stranger, and even if he did, he isn't going to tell him the secrets of his success. Here's the thing. Firstly, if you don't ask, the answer is always no. Secondly, you know we dis-cussed beliefs earlier in this guide, well something we didn't cover was the belief in abundance. Just about all the truly successful people I've met believe in abundance. In other words, they think there is too much to go round. Whether that's money or for that matter advice. They also believe that what they give away comes back to them tenfold. It's the universal principle of sowing and reaping once again in action. What do failures believe in? Limits. To them success is like a cake – if I give some to you, that's less for me. Anyway, you'll know if you've asked the right person for advice because they will be more than happy to tell you (they also under-stand the value of being a mentor, as covered in step ten).

Anyway, Richard made the call and guess what? Tom picked up the phone. Richard explained he had just the one shop but a big vision and loads of belief. He just wasn't sure about how to get started. Tom said: 'Come and see me. I'll tell you everything I know.' *Everything!*

I also once asked Desmond Lynam, television's Mr Cool: 'Can I ask your advice, how do you do that? How do you stay so relaxed, professional and charming on live television, even when every-thing is going wrong?' Des said two interesting things. Firstly, 'No one has ever asked me that before' and secondly, 'I've no idea.' You see, he didn't. Most peak performers are unconsciously com-petent. In other words, they do things in a state of flow without having to think about them. So I said to Des: 'I know you don't

YOU'LL KNOW IF you've asked the right person for advice because they will be more than happy to tell you.

know, but if you did, what would you say?' And then just looked at him expectantly. That was enough to bring some of his strategy to the surface. Now all this happened whilst we were having our photographs taken – Des was compere and I was a speaker at a conference – so I only got five minutes of his time. However, he did tell me three important things that he'd learned in his many years of live broadcasting. Does this mean I can be Des Lynam? No, but it did give me a distinct advantage, and made things seem a lot less daunting, the first time I was on live television.

Of course, you might not meet a role model. Trouble is, if you're not careful, that still doesn't stop you acting like someone else. You only need to have seen them, not even in the flesh, and know a little bit about them, for you to benefit from their experience. Here is a lesson in what can happen if you don't think about this. I was once asked to be a presenter on a sales video being filmed in an electrical superstore. Now this called for me to use an autocue for the first time (this is where the words appear in the camera, so you can read them without it looking like you are reading – just like newsreaders use). On the day of the shoot several things conspired to make me feel very uncomfortable and nervous. Firstly, no one told me the store would be open and would be full of customers, all staring at me. Secondly, just before we shot the first scene, the director asked me if I could make sure I hit all my marks. These were places marked on the floor to indicate where I should stop and, for instance, casually lean on a washing machine (the challenge with this is to do it without looking at the floor). Then he added, could I deliver my lines without my Yorkshire accent as the client didn't like it. (Now this is a bit like casting Arnold Schwarzenegger and asking him to sound like Laurence Olivier.) And of course can I still do all this without it looking like I'm reading and have never used an autocue before.

So, as I stood there waiting for them to shout 'Action', I'm sorry but I couldn't help but think, 'Who do I know who is outstanding at doing this?' Carol Vorderman immediately pops into mind (if you don't know who Carol is, you have obviously never watched any British TV programme – she is in most of them). I know Carol in person, which helps, and have seen her many times on TV using autocue. I imagined stepping inside Carol's body (not an unpleasant thought). As I did this I felt like I was looking out through her eyes and experiencing what was happening as she would experience it. Why did this help? Well, the first thing I thought was, 'I'm the great Carol Vorderman, why aren't more people looking at me?' and 'Is this all they want me to do? What a breeze, I'll get this in one take.' That helped me relax and get through without appearing an inexperienced idiot.

I IMAGINED stepping

inside Carol's body
(not an **unpleasant**
thought).

Jonathan Elvidge, the founder of the Gadget Shop, told me he also thought sometimes being naïve is a huge asset when it comes to life, work and business. He said because he didn't come from a retail background he had no preconceptions about how to go about opening his first store. So when people said things couldn't be done, he just thought 'why not?' and did them anyway.

Indeed, someone once told me that I would never make a profit running big seminars. 'I should know,' he said, 'because I work for one of the best-known seminar providers in the world. What with the huge cost of marketing, plus expensive venues, we never made any money except through sales of books, tapes and the like at the back of the room. That's the only reason we do it.' I'm glad he told me this when he did because by then we'd been holding large-scale, highly profitable seminars for over four years. And that was without having anything to sell at the back of the room. If I'd known what he knew before deciding to run our first seminar, I doubt we would have dared take the risk. We just didn't know you weren't meant to make money doing it.

Finally, what about the story of the Ford motor car dealer? Seemingly, in the early days, when all Ford sold was open-topped Model Ts, all dealers throughout America were told to close during the winter. Ford reasoned that you just wouldn't be able to sell open-topped cars at this inclement time of year. During the winter break, Henry Ford himself decided to do a tour of his most successful dealers to see how he could help them when they reopened in the summer. Arriving during a heavy snow storm at his most successful dealership – a place that sold nearly twice as many cars as everyone else – Ford was surprised to find it open. He at once summoned the manager and asked him what he thought he was doing selling cars in the middle of winter. The manager replied: 'Sorry, Mr Ford, nobody ever told us we had to close.'

Action not to take

Don't find someone who is outstanding at what they do. Someone who can do something to a level you can't yet reach but would like to. Don't go up to them and first say, 'Can I ask your advice?' You see, this person is, more than likely, going to be a complete stranger to you because, if it's somebody that outstanding, it won't be one of your current circle of friends. (Remember, you become who you spend most of your time with – there isn't much your mates can tell you that you don't already know.) If you ask a stranger for advice, they are more likely to be open to your request simply because we like being asked for our advice. 'Can I ask your advice?' 'No, bugger off.' In years of asking this I've never had that happen. If you insist on doing what I've told you not to do, don't follow up with the line '. . . and can I take notes?'

If you've never done something before, don't act 'as if' you have. Don't pretend to be someone else, over and over again. You may end up being as good as them. Or as Milton Erikson said 'pretend you can do anything then master it'. Most folks want to do it the other way round.

And please don't be so naïve. If you don't know that you can't do something, you will be stupid enough to go out and try, and you may find out you can. In fact, you may end up doing it better than your rivals for the very reason that you don't know how they do it.

Step thirty-two
Don't change the meaning of things.

Quote to avoid

'*I can't say I was ever lost, but I sure was bewildered for three days.*'

Daniel Boone

Before you read this letter the situation is as follows: It is 1920s America, and a boyfriend decides to buy his girlfriend a surprise present with the help of her sister. Secretly they go shopping together and visit a large department store. The sister tries on a long pair of silk fur-lined gloves and the boyfriend buys them. Before she leaves the store the sister also buys a long pair of silk knickers. Unfortunately the gloves and knickers are mixed up whilst being gift-wrapped. The girlfriend receives the knickers together with this note from her boyfriend:

My Dearest,

I hope you like the enclosed birthday present. Your sister helped me pick these out. She tried them on for me and I have to say they looked great although being so long they did prove difficult to get off.

Don't worry about the pale colour, the shop assistant showed me hers, that she had been wearing for several weeks, and they were hardly soiled at all.

However, the assistant did say that whenever you take them off, you should blow into them because they are bound to be a little damp after wearing.

I do wish I could be with you for your birthday, as I would love to put them on for you...I guess by the time I meet you on Saturday many other hands will have touched them.

Love Robert

PS Oh, the shop assistant also says that the latest fashion is to wear them rolled down with a little fur showing.

It's now impossible to travel anywhere by car without getting into a traffic jam. Knowing this fact, at the start of any long journey I'll call into the first service station and buy myself a treat. In my case this is usually a comedy CD (you could choose anything, it might be music or even a chocolate bar). The deal is, I'm not allowed the treat until I get into a traffic jam. Now, because I'm desperate to listen to my new comedy CD, sometimes I find myself praying for a jam. 'Yes, there's one,' I cry. 'Oh no, it's just traffic queuing for the slip road.' I find myself actually disappointed that there's no jam, imagine that. I have to wait and the excitement mounts. Then at last, inevitably, I hit a jam. 'Fantastic,' I think as I reach for my CD with a broad smile on my face. Then I look around me at the miserable-looking, frustrated faces of the other drivers.

Or what about this? Think about your favourite anecdote involving you. You know, the story you always tell in the pub that has everyone laughing their heads off. Now, as you think about that incident, I'm guessing it probably involved some disaster. Like the time you went on holiday, arrived at your destination and the airline had lost all your bags. Then on the way to your hotel the taxi driver ripped you off. You got out of the taxi and were immediately mugged and lost all your money. When you tried to check into your hotel, they hadn't reserved you a room and were fully booked. Finally, you ended up sleeping on a park bench and when you woke up in the morning, someone had stolen your shoes. The thing is, if it's so funny now, why wasn't it funny when it happened? It seems to me if you are going to have a big laugh at it later, why not reduce your stress levels and laugh at it as it actually happens.

THE THING IS, if it's so

funny now,

why wasn't it funny **when it happened?**

The point is, it's possible to change the meaning of absolutely anything that happens to us, simply by changing, or reframing, its context (the letters at the beginning and end of this step are great examples of what I mean). For instance, look at the shape below and I'd like you to tell me if it's concave or convex:

The answer of course is that it's both. It just depends which side you look at it from. Successful people, and companies for that matter, are very good at tolerating ambiguity and at seeing things from both sides. Everything is context dependent. It is possible to change the meaning of just about anything or to find the good where others would only find the bad. Of course, it should be your goal to stay a right misery, at all times, but especially when things go wrong. Naturally I wouldn't dream of saying, 'Is your glass half empty or half full?' because as good old Sam Goldwyn said: 'Give me some new clichés.' Besides, being from Yorkshire I'm not so much interested in the glass as whose round it is.

The point is better made with this letter sent by a college student to her parents:

Dear Mum and Dad,

Apologies for taking so long to write but my writing utensils were destroyed in a fire at my flat. I'm out of hospital now and the doctor says I should be able to lead a normal healthy life. A handsome young man called Pete saved me from the fire...and kindly offered to share his house with me. He's very kind and polite and from a good family...so I think you'll approve when I tell you we got married last week...and I know you'll be even more excited when I tell you, you are going to be grandparents very soon.

Actually, there wasn't a fire, I haven't been in hospital, I'm not married and I'm not pregnant, BUT I did fail my maths exam and I just wanted to make sure that when I told you that you'd put it in the proper perspective.

Your loving daughter

Sue

Action not to take

Don't instantly change what things mean to you simply by looking at them in a different way. As comedian Billy Connolly says: 'There is no such thing as bad weather, just the wrong clothes.' Talking of which, here are my two favourite examples of how most jokes work by changing the context:

'So I was getting into my car, and this bloke says to me, "Can you give me a lift?" I said, "Sure, you look great, the world's your oyster, go for it."'

Tim Vine gets the credit for that gem. Whereas this beauty comes from the mind of Milton Jones:

'I was walking down the street and I saw a dead baby ghost in the road. On reflection, it might have been a handkerchief.'

Don't take responsibility for how you want to feel about things in advance of them actually happening. Or after they have happened. For example, when something goes wrong don't ask: 'How can I use this?' Or when someone walks into your office and, out of the blue, resigns, don't use a context-changing question like, 'What's great about this problem?' to generate lots of possible solutions. Don't stop groaning, 'Oh no, what are we going to do, how will we ever replace them?' over and over again.

Step thirty-three

Don't stop thinking only about money, money, money.

Quote to avoid

'If money is your hope for independence, you will never have it. The only real security that a man can have in this world is a reserve of knowledge, experience and ability.' **Henry Ford**

Here is something I read in the newspaper the other day: 'It is often said that money can't buy happiness, although there are plenty of hard-up people who find it hard to believe. Now psychologists claim to have the proof. A study has found that being rich and beautiful has little to do with overall contentment. Instead, it concluded that we are happiest when we feel in charge of our own lives; have high self-esteem; enjoy a close network of friends and family; and believe we are doing well, rather than being incompetent or ineffective. To reach their conclusions, the psychologists at the University of Missouri-Columbia interviewed 700 students in the US and Korea. The students were asked their most satisfying experiences. They were then asked to explain why these events had made them happy. Money was mentioned least as a reason. "Being true to yourself"; being competent at activities; having close bonds with other people; and feeling respect for yourself topped the list.'

What lessons are there in this for the serious student of failure? Well, firstly, we must forget that wealth isn't about money. Just concentrate on what you'd like to have, material things like money, cars or other 'objects'. This is guaranteed to pull you away from feeling the way you want to feel. Especially when you get some stuff and it still doesn't make you happy or content.

As well as forgetting that money doesn't buy you happiness, failures also believe in scarcity. They'd agree with the sentiment that 'money talks . . . but all mine ever says is goodbye'. They believe that things, including money, are like a cake – there are only so many pieces and if I give some away to you, that's going to be less for me. Successful people believe in the exact opposite – abundance. That there is too much to go around and the more I give away, the more comes back to me. They believe money is in never-ending supply. That the world is awash with the stuff. The secret is that they don't chase it. Have you noticed that the more you chase money, the more it runs away? No, they know profit is a consequence of being the best you can be and doing the thing you love to do. Because they are not in it for the money, unlike you, they don't quit at the first obstacle that's put in their way.

HAVE YOU noticed that
the more you chase money,
the more it runs
away?

Action not to take

Money is an important aspect of success, especially if you believe the best way to help the poor is not to be one of them. Financial independence gives you control. You can choose what you want to do and not do. However, failures think the best way to get their hands on some of the folding stuff is through a large dollop of luck. They cross their fingers and hope. In the extremely unlikely event that their number does come up, ironically that will just be the beginning of their problems. You see, 80% of lottery winners lose all their money within five years. That's because they didn't believe they deserved it in the first place. You, however, if you want to keep your bank account in the red, mustn't believe you need to be wealthy in your head before you can be wealthy in your life.

Someone once said: 'When it comes to giving to others, I stop at nothing.' Successful people know the best way to reduce money's power over you is by regularly giving some of it away. Strangely, the best time to do this is when you don't have much of the stuff yourself. Same thing goes for paying bills. Most people moan and groan when they have to write out a cheque for the gas bill. They attach a sort of negative energy to the whole activity. Successful people, meanwhile, pay with a smile on their face. They believe in an abundant universe where whatever goes out must come back in spades, often from the most unexpected quarters. You must not believe this if your goal is to remain poor.

So remember, don't think about what you want to be, then do, then have. Just think about the money.

Step thirty-four
Don't have a good laugh.

Quote to avoid

'Smile well and often, it makes people wonder what you've been up to.'

Satchel Paige

Picture two skinny, hungry-looking vultures up a tree in the middle of the African plains. There's not another creature for as far as the eye can see. One vulture looks at the other and says: 'Never mind be patient, I'm going to go kill something.' The point of the joke is that sometimes we have to take action if we are going to survive. You, of course, must ignore this advice.

However, our topic in this step is humour. In the UK, and I guess many other places too, I've noticed people are suffering from terminal seriousness, especially at work. And a good thing too. Do you really think it's possible to do a good job and have a laugh in the process? Of course not. You've got to keep your nose to the grindstone and keep that stupid big smile off your big fat face. Still, that shouldn't be too difficult as most people hate their jobs with a vengeance. As Thoreau said: 'The mass of men lead lives of quiet desperation.' For most people, surely the only reason to smile at work is on the day you retire.

The same goes for training and education. The evidence overwhelmingly shows that if learning is made fun, we not only enjoy it more but also remember more. If we're not careful, people will want to go off on courses willy-nilly, and as you'll see from step thirty-nine, we don't want them or you doing that. On average children laugh at least 40 times a day, whereas adults laugh a mere 15. I think this proves that kids are buffoons and the sooner they shape up and stop seeing the funny side of just about everything, the better. Megan, aged 11, told me this joke the other day: 'What's ET short for? Because he's got little legs.'

No matter that science has shown that when we laugh, and it doesn't even have to be a great big belly laugh, we increase the amount of endorphins in the body (these are the body's natural happy drug and are totally legal and free). Not only that, but through laughter we boost the body's immune system and thereby keep ourselves healthier. Robert Provine, professor of psychology and neuroscience at the University of Maryland and author of the best-selling book *Laughter: A Scientific Investigation*, says experts are only just beginning to understand the extent to which injections of humour can have potent benefits for body and mind. In adults, laughter has been shown to cut the risk of heart disease, and not just because it reduces pent-up tension. When colleagues of Provine at the University of Maryland questioned 150 healthy people and 150 people who had suffered a heart attack or undergone bypass surgery, they found that those with heart disease were less inclined to laugh, even in positive situations. What researchers suspect is that regular laughter prevents damage to the endothelium, the protective barrier lining our blood vessels. When this is

IN ADULTS, laughter has been shown to cut the risk of heart disease, and not just because it reduces pent-up tension.

impaired, as it is with too much stress, it is thought to trigger an inflammatory reaction that causes fat and cholesterol to build up in the arteries. 'Regular hearty laughter should be added to exercise and a low-fat diet as a means of lowering the risk of heart disease,' says Dr Michael Miller, one of the Maryland scientists. 'We should try to stop taking ourselves so seriously.'

The results from a five-year study at the School of Medicine, University of California Los Angeles (UCLA), also show that a fit of the giggles really could be the best medicine. This study proved that when sick children laughed, there was a significant improvement in pain management and the body's natural defences, as well as a direct response of the autonomic nervous system responsible for involuntary action, which can be damaged by illness.

In fact, so convincing is the evidence supporting the value of a good laugh, don't be surprised if at some time in the future your doctor writes you a prescription for two comedy videos to be taken first thing in the morning and last thing at night. We also know the quickest way to change your mood, or state, is to put a big smile on your face. As far as your body and brain are concerned, if you're smiling you must be happy, and so that's how you'll feel. That's why you must never stop having a cold, miserable, poker face at all times. Why not throw in a few 'Ba, humbugs' for good measure?

Action not to take

Some things are unintentionally funny, like the instructions on the deodorant stick which said, 'Unscrew top and push up bottom,' so it's hard not to laugh. However, don't deliberately plan things that will make you laugh, like listening to comedy tapes (especially if it makes you crack up more than 40 times a day). Don't notice how easy kids find it to fall about on the floor laughing their silly little heads off.

Step thirty-five
Don't be creative or innovative.

Quote to avoid

'Creative thinking may mean simply the realization that there is no particular virtue in doing things the way they have always been done.' **Rudolph Flesch**

Talking about not having a good laugh, this is also a prerequisite if you don't want to be innovative or creative. You mustn't ever make work fun, even though Tom Peters says: 'Not to have fun at work is a tragedy, bordering on the criminal. Curiosity and fun are hand-maidens. Go out of your way to make laughter a workplace staple.' You see, there's no way you can come up with quicker, better, more cost-effective, innovative ways of achieving your goals, no way you can improve your life, job, company, products or services, if you aren't curious. Don't ever challenge the status quo.

I spent 15 years working in advertising as a creative director. Now, if at a party I inadvertently let this slip, I would typically get one of four responses:

➡ 'Why don't they just take all those millions they spend on advertising off the price of the product?'

➡ 'You exploit women.'

➡ 'Did you do that fantastic ad for (insert your favourite commercial here)?'

➡ 'I don't know how you do that. Sit there all day and wait for those wacky ideas to appear in light bulbs above your head. Knowing that if you can't think of anything you will be fired. I don't believe I could do that!'

To which my answers would be:

→ 'Yeah, then you'd still know what was out there and where to buy it.'

→ 'Yes.' (This response was always guaranteed to liven up a boring party.)

→ 'No.'

→ 'Ah well, that is a fallacy fostered by characters like Darren who played the part of an advertising executive in the popular TV show *Bewitched*. You see, we had lots of strategies. Many of which we got from copying other creative people or out of the loads of books on innovation and creativity readily available at your public library or these days on the Internet.'

You must not stop thinking that people are either creative or they are not. At school you were educated out of creativity into judgement. Don't think this is reversible.

AT SCHOOL you were educated out of creativity into judgement. Don't think this is reversible.

Action not to take

A few years ago I kept finding mud all over the bathroom towel. Putting two and two together I suspected the culprit might be second son Finlay who was about four at the time. When I confronted him with the evidence, he said: 'Well, where else am I supposed to wipe my boomerang?' A phrase I have never heard in conversation before or since. Creativity is all about being childlike and suggesting unexpected answers to the challenging questions you face. My friend, and fellow speaker, Sir Ken Robinson tells the following story to demonstrate the innate creativity of children: 'A teacher is going around the classroom looking at the children's paintings. She gets to one little five-year-old girl and says, "And what are you drawing?" The child replies, "Miss, it's a picture of God." "But nobody knows what God looks like," says the teacher. "They will in a minute," says the little girl.'

So let me ask you: 'Were you once a child?' (Show me a child without an imagination.) 'Do you dream?' (Boy, just look at some of the colourful, amazing things you come up with.) Please don't let these two facts stop you believing you're not creative. Don't learn about and explore the process of creativity and innovation. Walt Disney thought of it this way: 'Somehow I can't believe there are many heights that can't be scaled by a man who knows the secret of making dreams come true. This special secret, it seems to me, can be summarized in the four Cs. Curiosity, confidence, courage and consistency.' And what's the best way to believe you are creative? Just decide right this moment that from now on you are. So don't do that, will you?

Step thirty-six

Don't think of your own idea to go here.

Quote to avoid

'A new idea is delicate. It can be killed by a sneer or a yawn; it can be stabbed to death by a quip, and worried to death by the frown on the right man's brow.'

Charlie Brower

If you know someone who can come up with an extra idea on failure to go here, please let me know (my contact details can be found on the inside back cover of this guide). I'm guessing if you're reading this then it won't be you. By the way, if you're unlucky enough to have a bright spark within your organization or life (by definition they won't have been with you long), don't stop using any of the following responses in order to kill their ideas: 'We tried it before'; 'That sounds crazy to me'; 'Maybe next year'; 'It would cost too much time and/or money'; 'Our customers would never go for that'; 'You can't do that here'; 'Get out of my office'; or 'You're fired'. Don't think my reaction to any of your ideas would be open-minded interest either.

Of course, if in the unlikely event you're the one having the ideas, you might do well to note Howard Aiken's advice: 'Don't worry about people stealing an idea. If it's original, you will have to ram it down their throats.'

Here's a tip for making the least of your ideas. If you can't avoid a brainstorming session, and please do your best to do so, then don't ever brainstorm past one or two ideas at the most. Simply settle for the first bland, boring or safe idea that pops into your head. Remember that research into creativity and innovation has shown if you push past 20 or more ideas, aiming for say a minimum of 40, it is often these later ideas that are more valuable. Sometimes you'll find if you combine these later, often crazy ideas with some of your early, more obvious ones, you can create some stunning solutions to the problems and challenges you face. But as I've said, the best way to avoid this is to have no ideas at all.

SIMPLY SETTLE for the

first bland, boring or safe idea that

pops into

your head.

my idea on how to be more of a failure/success is

don't dare write anything here

Step thirty-seven

Don't stop always taking 'no' for an answer.

Quote to avoid

'I realized early on that success was tied to not giving up. Most people in this business gave up and went on to other things. If you simply didn't give up, you would outlast the people who came in on the bus with you.' **Harrison Ford**

David Zucker said: 'Quit now, you'll never make it. If you disregard this advice, you'll be halfway there.' He may be right. Research in the field of selling has shown that 73% of customers say 'no' five or more times before they say 'yes'. By five or more times, I mean after a phone call, a meeting, or say upon receiving some of your marvellous marketing material which is immediately filed in the bin.

The good news is that such is our fear of rejection that most of us won't even give something or someone new one try (note: these figures relate just as much to your disastrous attempts at dating members of the opposite sex as they do to selling).

So being committed to failure, and as someone who quits even before they start, as I know you are, of course you won't even have to worry about picking up the phone in the first place. But if you do, accidentally, build up the courage to try once and hear the dreaded 'no', then at least that's it. You can put your hand on your heart and say you gave it your best shot.

Just don't let your boss, or anyone else, find out that according to this research only 8% of salespeople go past five 'no's'. Which means they are getting 73% of the business. This naturally makes them the most successful individuals in the organization and guarantees the rewards that go with that. Of course, their belief is that if you don't ask, the answer is always 'no'. Dr Joyce Brothers says this: 'Studies indicate that the one quality all successful people have is persistence. They're willing to spend more time accomplishing a task and to persevere in the face of many difficult odds. There's a very positive relationship between people's ability to accomplish any task and the time they're willing to spend on it.'

Want to know what I think? Well, I think they are just masochists and the best thing we can do to protect our sensitive dispositions is be realistic (which is just another word for scared). I mean, it isn't going to be very encouraging to be able to say to yourself, 'Whoopee, I just got a fourth "no", just one more and the business is mine,' is it?

Action not to take

Don't commit to becoming unstoppable. Don't breathe, stand, move or talk like someone who is unstoppable. Don't try, try and try again. Don't even take 'yes' for an answer. Don't consider William James's observation that 'most people never run far enough on their first wind to find out if they've got a second. Give your dreams all you've got and you'll be amazed at the energy that comes out of you.'

Step thirty-eight
Don't be grateful.

Quote to avoid

' In our minds, we must see that it is not happiness that makes us grateful, but rather gratefulness that makes us happy. ' **Albert Clark**

The surveys say that moving house is one of the most stressful things you can do. We want the new house so, so much and are fearful that at any time things could fall through that we spend all our energy focusing on what we could lose instead of remembering what we already have. What we know from modelling failures is that they very rarely, if ever, take time to be grateful for what they already have, and instead moan about what they don't have. It's like the cartoon strip *Peanuts* which once showed Charlie Brown playing with half of a broken yo-yo. We see him having a great time playing fetch with his dog Snoopy. Then Charlie Brown's girlfriend Lucy appears. 'You stupid dummy,' she says. 'You can't have a good time with half a yo-yo. Everybody knows that.' The dejected Charlie Brown throws the broken toy away. 'I'm sorry,' replies the little boy. 'I didn't know I couldn't enjoy myself with a broken yo-yo.'

Whereas successful individuals take time, now and again, to count their blessings. So, for example, if they start to feel frustrated or stressed, say by the lack of movement on a house move, they content themselves with this thought: 'If someone took away absolutely everything I have right now, would I be grateful to have it all back? You bet.' No matter how little you feel you have to be grateful for, I guarantee it will always be more than having nothing. Being grateful for what you have helps release you from what can seem like a problem or disappointment. That is because gratitude acknowledges what works instead of what doesn't.

NO MATTER how little **you feel** you have to **be grateful for,** I guarantee it will **always be more** than **having nothing.**

Not only that, but gratefulness can be used as a means of attracting what you want in your life. World peace expert James Twyman says this: 'When we ask for something to happen, the attention is on the fact that we don't have it now. But when we feel that it has already occurred, then we put out an energy that actually draws that reality to us. Gratitude is a key element. It is very important to be grateful.' So if you want to push things away from you, don't regularly ask yourself the following questions and don't make a list of all the answers: 'How can I allow myself to be grateful?' 'Who am I grateful for in my life?' 'What am I grateful for in my life?' Not asking questions like this helps you to stay negative because you're looking for the bad instead of the good. And as you already know, we always find what we're looking for.

One day in 2004 not very long after the terrible Boxing Day Tsunami had struck, and a couple of weeks before his twelfth birthday, Finlay (yes, the boomerang kid is back in the guide again) was moping about at home looking miserable. I asked him what was wrong and he said, 'It's my birthday soon and my life sucks.' So I said, 'Why don't you write down on a piece of paper everything that is troubling you.' He agreed and several minutes later, with a glum look on his face, he handed me this letter:

To Mum and Dad

glasses not clean.

No friends that have the same interests as me.

getting bad presents from realtives.

The amount of homework I get.

How I am bored all the time (can we please do something at a weekend).

People always swearing at me when I walk home.

Tom being irratiting.

tom calling me 'fat boy'.

No-one showing little interest in my magic.

How I can't meet other people and go places I want (is it REALLY THAT MUCH to ask?)

How no one pays attention when I am speaking at tea time.

How they are no pens in the house (note that I'm writing in pencil).

Can you try to do something?

PS These are 1/4 of my problems

Now upon reading this several thoughts occurred to me:

➡ The reason that there are no glasses to drink from is because they are all under Finlay's bed.

➡ Bad presents from relatives. I think he means some of the aunties and uncles will forget, because they don't see him that often, that he is no longer five years old and will buy him unsuitable presents. He'll then have to smile and pretend he likes what they have bought him. Wait till he starts getting socks for Christmas.

➡ I'm not exactly coming out of this as Super Dad on the keep me entertained front.

➡ People swearing at him. That was worth finding out, must investigate.

➡ Glad I didn't have an older brother growing up.

➡ I watch his magic tricks for hours on end and always engage him in conversation when we have a meal together (that's one of the reasons we do it). Doesn't matter, his perception is that I'm not interested. Must work harder at this.

➡ At last he's running out of things to moan about and has had to resort to the 'can't find a pen' angle.

➡ Blimey these are only a few of his problems, was I like this when I was his age?

I then said to Finlay, 'OK, now go write a list of things you can be grateful for.' This is what he came back with moments later, including the unusual spelling (it wasn't very long but it was in ink so at least he'd now found a pen):

A loving family.

A Decent (well more than decent) house and possessions.

Not bieing dead in the Tsunami.

Bieing lucky to live in peace.

I took one look at what he'd written and, with a big lump in my throat, thought: 'Thanks Finlay for pointing out to me some of the things I take for granted.' I felt very grateful indeed. So I said to Finlay, 'Having done that little exercise has it made you feel any better?' to which he replied, 'Do you know Dad, it definitely has.' Do you think he really said that? Of course not. He actually said, 'That was the biggest waste of time ever.' The thing is, at the time he was 11 years old. You're not.

Action not to take

Don't live with an attitude of gratitude. On those days that you think you don't have anything to be happy about, don't listen to Ian Dury and The Blockheads' great song 'Reasons to be Cheerful'. It will change your mood. Don't see if you can list 100 things, big and small, you can be grateful for (if you did, you'd be surprised that it's easy to go way past 100 – unless of course you are 11 years old). Don't see everyday exchanges as opportunities to express gratitude. For example, don't thank a waiter who has served you well, and don't make a point of telling their manager how grateful you are that he employs such good people. After all, it's not your job to make complete strangers feel good, is it? It won't make you feel better, will it?

Step thirty-nine
Don't commit to lifelong learning.

Quote to avoid

'Progress might have been all right once, but it's gone on too long.'

Ogden Nash

Most of the successful people I've met invest 5%, often much more, of their annual income on their own development (books, CDs, training courses). Whereas you should spend your money on a new car rather than invest it in yourself. What's the point of committing to lifelong learning when there are so many other wonderful things you could do with your hard-earned cash? Here is one reason, as expressed by Benjamin Franklin: 'If a man empties his purse into his head, no man can take it away from him. An investment in knowledge always pays the best interest.' Yes, but is it as much fun as leaping behind the wheel of your new car?

Experts claim increasing your knowledge not only plays a crucial role in your development as a person, it is also a key component of achieving your goals. They say it stands to reason you are going to have to gain more knowledge and learn new skills. Otherwise you would already have achieved the goal. Then of course there is the speed of change. The same experts reckon the jobs my three children will have when they leave school don't exist yet. They say there doesn't seem much point in only teaching them stuff like 'What was the name of Edward VI's whipping boy?'[1] (It's Barnaby Fitzpatrick by the way.) No, if our kids are to survive

---

[1] They weren't allowed to hit the king if he misbehaved at school so instead they whipped poor old Barnaby.

in the high-speed world of the future, every lesson first thing on a Monday morning should be called 'Learning how to learn'. Still, that's got nothing to do with us adults, unless you believe Brian Tracy, an authority on accelerated learning, who says: 'Fifty per cent of what you know now will be obsolete in two years' time. That is why school is never out. To earn more you must learn more.' And so what if, as Henry Ford once said, 'Anyone who stops learning is old, whether at 20 or 80. Anyone who keeps learning stays young'?

Have you also noticed how employers now expect you to improve year on year? The cheek of it. I knew somebody who worked somewhere for ten years but in reality got away with delivering the same one year's performance ten times. Nice one. Unfortunately not possible any longer. You are going to have to prove your improvement. Still, don't stop being satisfied with knowing just enough to get by.

Of course, if you're the boss, you might be thinking, 'What if I train people and they leave?' to which you might reply, 'What if

YOU ARE GOING to have to prove your improvement. Still, don't stop being satisfied with knowing just enough to get by.

you don't train them and they stay?' I'd just leave their brains to shrivel slowly to the size of a pea.

Here is something else not to file away if you are a boss or a parent. (Can you be a boss and a parent? Not as far as your kids are concerned.) People will lower or raise their performance based on expectations. Trials have shown that, for instance, in the world of education high expectations build competence, low expectations instil incompetence. Known as the Pygmalion effect, a test was conducted to see whether expectations really would colour results. Three teachers were selected and told they were the best in the education authority and therefore were to be given three classes of the brightest and most able students. The three classes of students were also told they were of higher ability. The three teachers taught their three classes for a full school year. At the end the pupils sat exams. All three classes performed well above average. Only then was it revealed that in fact the three teachers were of only average ability and so were the three classes. So what had happened to create such an improvement? Well, fundamentally, all behaviour had been interpreted through the perception of higher ability. So whereas a child might have been seen as being disruptive, now they were seen as eager to learn and quickly bored. It's a proven fact: expect the best or the worst and that's just what you'll get. What do you usually expect?

Action not to take

Don't have the attitude of the self-employed (if you work full time for one company, don't pretend you just have one important client – them). Don't regularly ask: 'What do I know that I didn't know last year?' Don't ask: 'What will I need to know to succeed in five years' time?' and then start learning about it now. Just live in a house with a sign outside saying 'Dunlearning'.

Ignore Mario Andretti, who although he was into leaping behind the wheel of a new car – he was, after all, a professional racing driver – also valued the need for never-ending improvement. Andretti believed the best time to learn is often just after a setback. 'Even though circumstances may cause interruptions and delays, never lose sight of your goal. Instead, prepare yourself in every way you can by increasing your knowledge and adding to your experience, so that you can make the most of opportunity when it occurs.'

Great expectations isn't just the title of a book, it's also a successful person's view of life. However, as someone once said: 'Readers are leaders.' So hopefully you've never heard of it. Mind you Noël Coward also had a point: 'You live and learn. Then you die and forget it all.'

Step forty
Don't be a leader.

Quote to avoid

'Do not walk behind me, for I may not lead. Do not walk ahead of me, for I may not follow. Do not walk beside me, either…just leave me the hell alone.'

Anon

When I was 13 years old something happened that, with the benefit of hindsight, was a life-changing event – and no, it wasn't my first kiss. I was in the Scouts and we were camping on the coast near Morecambe. One day a football match was organized between our troop and another scout troop who were camped down the road. As we were walking to the game on a beautiful summer's day with not a cloud in the sky our Scout Master, Mr Walsh, turned to me and casually said, 'Steve, you're captain for this match, make sure the lads give it their best shot and have a good time.' Now it might have sounded like a throw-away line from Mr Walsh (in fact I subsequently discovered he'd actually given it a great deal of thought), but to me this was to say the least surprising, earth shattering, joyous news. Suddenly without warning this had become the best day of my life. You see, unless you've been a 13-year-old football mad boy you might not get this. At that age, playing football was everything. That's EVERYTHING. But being captain – that was everything plus one.

At the time England were still World Cup holders and my all-time hero was England captain Bobby Moore. If you'll pardon the pun, more than anything else I wanted to be Moore. Now just like my hero I had been made captain of the side. Not only that, I played the same position as Bobby at the heart of defence. The only remaining difference between us was that he could read the game, time a tackle to perfection (who can forget his master class against Pele's Brazil in the 1970 World Cup?) and create a scoring chance from nothing with an inch perfect 50-yard pass.

But I simply couldn't do any of the things that Bobby could do. In fact, I couldn't do most of the things the other 13 year olds in my side appeared to do with ease. You see, although I might not admit it to my friends, deep down on the inside I'd come to the terrible conclusion that I'd never play for England. I knew this because I couldn't even get into the school side. Not that I didn't keep hoping that some miracle would take place. Perhaps, I told myself, I was just a late developer. Maybe, just maybe, I'd wake up one morning and suddenly be able to dribble like Best, shoot like Charlton and play 'keepy up' beyond three.[1] The only reason I made the Scouts side was that we were always short of numbers. Two legs were the only qualification you needed and it was OK if the two legs in question suffered from a lack of coordination, just as long as you could supply your own boots.

This is why, as we walked down that sun speckled country lane all those years ago, I was on the one hand elated and on the other confused. I mean, I knew I wasn't the absolute worst player in the team but I was far from the best (at least I never had the ultimate humiliation of being picked last from the line-up of usual suspects before a kick about). Why, totally out of the blue, would you pick me as captain? I came to the startling conclusion that Mr Walsh had seen something in me that I hadn't, up until that moment, seen in myself. He'd seen my potential as a leader. He

---

[1] 'Keepy up' – this is where you have to keep the football off the ground for as long as possible. According to *Guinness World Records*, the world record for football control belongs to Nikolai Kutsenko of Ukraine, who juggled a regulation soccer ball for $24^1/_2$ hours non-stop with feet, legs and head, without the ball ever touching the ground. Beats my 30 seconds by a considerable distance.

knew that the qualities that make an inspiring leader are very rarely just to do with being the best technically. As we approached the field selected as the venue for the match, which going by the smell had only very recently been vacated by a herd of cows – and you don't even want to think about what the cows had vacated – I made a solemn vow that I wouldn't let Mr Walsh, the team or myself down. Not only that, if this was to be my first, and possibly last, match as captain, I would lead by example. I might not be Bobby Moore, I might not be able to take his skills on to the pitch, but I could take his attitude and temperament on to the pitch. Although I was playing at the back I could lead from the front. I can't even remember if we won but what I do remember is that after that match things changed. For ever.

It turned out Mr Walsh was right. I captained the team for every match from then on. That one seminal event went on to colour the rest of my life. Not only did it build a strong, unshakeable foundation of confidence, but from that day to this it made me unafraid to step forward and take the lead, not wait to be selected, in many other areas of my life and subsequent careers. I've seized every opportunity to lead with both hands. For me leadership isn't a position, it's a mindset. You see, what I came to realize in that mucky cow field, and in the many other metaphorical mucky cow fields down the years since then, is that a leader is a dealer in hope. Even when it appears you are facing impossible odds, which frequently in life and work you are, the leader sees the light at the end of the tunnel and can get the team to glimpse it too. A true leader is a servant to the needs of the team. When Alexander the Great and his vast army were crossing the desert they stopped for a rest only to discover they were down to their last cup of water. When the cup was offered first to Alexander he took it and cast all of the water into the sand saying, 'Until we can all drink no one drinks.'

A TRUE LEADER is a
servant to the
needs of
the team.

Another good definition of a leader is someone who has earned the right to have followers. Here's something I came across concerning the characteristics of credible leaders:

→ They do what they say they will do. They keep their promises and follow through on their commitments.

→ Their actions are consistent with the wishes of the people they lead. They have a clear idea of what others value and what they can do.

→ They believe in the inherent self-worth of others.

→ They learn how to discover and communicate the shared values and visions that can form a common ground on which all can stand.

→ They are capable of making a difference in the lives of others – and liberating the leader in everyone.

→ They admit their mistakes. They realize that attempting to hide mistakes is much more damaging and erodes credibility. But when they admit a mistake, they do something about it.

→ They arouse optimistic feelings and enable their people to hold positive thoughts about the possibilities of success.

→ They create a climate for learning characterized by trust and openness.

So to remain rubbish at leading anything, including yourself, don't try to resemble any of the above.

Action not to take

Why would you ever want to be a leader anyway? By their very nature leaders are visionaries, and you already know that failures don't ever think about, or plan for, the future. That's why you don't want to step forward. The word leader comes from the old English word Laed – meaning path, road or journey. A leader accompanies people on a journey, guiding them to their destination. By implication he or she holds them together as a group. What better legacy could you leave than to have led your kids, family, friends or colleagues down the right path?

Leaders are also people who make things better, faster. And outstanding leaders make things a lot better, a lot faster. You don't want to earn a reputation for being able to do that. If you did, just imagine what rewards would follow and they wouldn't just be financial.

If someone else attempts to thrust you into the limelight resist at all costs. Hang back in the shadows. And if no one else spots it, don't see your own potential to become an outstanding leader. As Field Marshal Lord Slim put it: 'There is nobody who cannot vastly improve his powers of leadership by a little thought and practice.'

Another way of thinking about leadership is as the transfer of emotion. Let's say you're the boss, do you think that how you walk in in the morning is how your people will walk out last thing at night? Do you think the mood you're in will affect them? The answer is absolutely. And all this before most times you've even opened your mouth. A good way to evaluate the quality of the emotions you have transferred in the past, and therefore your quality of leadership, is to ask this question:

Would you say that people tend to react to you in a smiling, positive manner, giving you warm, friendly greetings when you appear? Or, in other words, are people glad to see you, or are they glad to see the back of you?

Oh dear!

Finally, if you are already a leader don't ever stop to ask, 'If I was one of my team, would I be loyal to me?'

Step forty-one

Don't learn to communicate.

Quote to avoid

'The trouble with her is that she lacks the power of conversation but not the power of speech.' **George Bernard Shaw**

Have you ever thought about this: you can't not communicate. That's right. Even if you stand there saying nothing you'll still be speaking volumes. Or as someone once said: 'What you are speaks so loudly that I can't hear what you are saying.' Here is a story to illustrate the point.[1]

I once attended a sales conference of two thousand delegates at the Wembley Conference Centre in London. The afternoon session kicked off with a presentation from an image consultant who, in order to protect his identity, I'll call Mr Pink. Image consultants are the kind of people who sidle up to you at parties and casually say, 'I

EVEN IF you stand
there saying
nothing you'll still
be speaking volumes.

[1] By the way, a great method for making things more memorable is to tell people personal stories. So instead of doing that, as a master of boredom, you must just stick to the bare facts. Oh, and have loads and loads of slides.

see you are wearing black, why?' to which you reply, 'Well because I like it.' And then they say, 'Yes, but does it like you?'

Mr Pink was one of the most professional presenters I had seen. As you would expect he was immaculately groomed and he knew his stuff. For instance, he never once looked around at the giant screen behind him because, unlike most amateurs, he wasn't using the slides as an aid to his memory. He began by saying there were lots of studies about what makes for clear, powerful communication, but that he'd like to concentrate on a piece of research from the University of Pennsylvania conducted by Professor Albert Mehrabian. Professor Mehrabian stated that the three major factors in communication are what we say, tone of voice and anything that isn't what we say or how we say it, or in other words your non-verbal communication. 'If these three factors added up to 100%,' Mr Pink then went on to say, 'what percentage out of 100%, in terms of your effectiveness as a communicator, would you give, first of all, to the words you use?'

Suddenly I realized that the fabulous Mr Pink wasn't quite as cool and professional as I had first thought. You see, at the very moment he asked us the question the answer appeared in 12-foot-high letters on the screen behind his head. I now realized he wasn't working the slides himself. Unfortunately, whoever he'd asked to work them on his behalf hadn't been told not to show the audience the answer until we'd had a chance to think about it. The thing is, Mr Pink had been trained never to turn around and look at his own slides, so he was blissfully ignorant of what had just happened.

At this point an amazing thing occurred. Do you believe we can all communicate with each other telepathically? Well now I had irrefutable proof that indeed this was possible, because at that exact moment all two thousand people seated in that auditorium had exactly the same thought, yet nobody spoke. The thought was, 'Don't tell him we can see the answer,' so we just sat there.

Mr Pink asked us the question again: 'So what do you think? What percentage in terms of your effectiveness as a communicator is down to the words you use?' Eventually a lone hand went up at the front of the room. 'Would it be 7%?' said the owner of the hand. 'That's absolutely correct. Tell me, have you heard these figures before?' asked a slightly taken-aback Mr Pink. 'Oh no, it was just a lucky guess,' lied the man in the audience. 'Anyway...' continued Mr Pink, 'when I first heard that I was surprised. I thought that it could not be possible that only 7% could be attributed to the "what" of communication. However, over many years' experience I have accepted that it is certainly a minimum part of communication.'

'So,' says Mr Pink, 'if you take 7 from 100 that leaves 93. Now we can divide this number between the two remaining communication factors. Now consider what percentage in terms of your effectiveness as a communicator is to do with "how" you say something or, if you like, your tone of voice.' Now once again the slide man had not been briefed and once again, quick as a flash, the answer appeared behind Mr Pink's head in letters 12 foot high. 'Any guesses?' enquires Mr Pink, at which point the mind melt reached its climax and right on cue two thousand voices shouted, 'WOULD IT HAPPEN TO BE 38%?' This had the effect of totally freaking out Mr Pink because he had no idea how we were doing this. He quickly garbled, '...so if you add 7 to 38 you'll realize a remaining whopping 55% of your communication is non-verbal, your physiology and body language'. Exit Mr Pink.

Now I'm sure many people have heard various experts quote these numbers before (I even saw them used in a TV ad). The thing to say here is not only was Mr Pink a bit of a plonker, but clearly it isn't as simple as he is making out. For example, if I'd said to him, 'Mr Pink, please tell me all that again but this time without slides and without speaking,' he'd have found it almost impossible.

However, these numbers are still important for two reasons. Firstly, they become critical when you are incongruent in your communication. Which is a fancy way of saying when stuff doesn't match. For example, when you say in a boring, monotone voice, 'I'm really excited about what I'm learning from reading Steve's book.' Clearly the tone of voice doesn't match the words. Secondly, the numbers are important in terms of the overall impact you make on others.

What has all this got to do with being a failure? Well you see, it's really important that you don't think about the way you communicate. That way next time you have an important message to get across to your boss, partner, team or even bank manager, you'll spend all your time worrying about what you are going to say rather than thinking how you can make a more lasting, overall impression by the way you say it. Or indeed the way you look or move (a friend who works for a city firm told me, 'I don't dress for the job I have now, I dress for the job I want to have'). This means you haven't much chance of convincing anyone of anything. And this is just one of the hundreds of secrets of knowing what it takes to be a great communicator. You see, it's no coincidence that Harvard Business School has identified the number one skill you need, to rise to the top of a company, is an ability to speak powerfully and persuasively in public.

Action not to take

All successful people know they cannot achieve anything of lasting value on their own. They know they are going to have to persuade and involve others to help them. For instance, they figure it's absolutely no good having a great vision for the future if you can't articulate it to others and get them excited and inspired about coming along for the ride. That's why they are constantly working on improving their communication skills. They have realized that becoming a great speaker, writer or listener[2] is something you can learn to do. They understand that these skills are not something you are lucky enough to be born with, as most folk would like to believe, but can be learnt and built upon throughout your life. They have unlocked the secrets through study, training, practice and modelling the great communicators that can be found all around us, from stand-up comedians to politicians[3] or even celebrity cooks.

Because they believe there is no such thing as failure, only feedback, successful individuals confront the fear of speaking in public head on. Running towards every opportunity they can get, or

BECAUSE they believe there is no such thing as failure, only feedback, successful individuals confront the fear of speaking in public head on.

[2] When most people think of communication they tend to ignore the ability to listen. In fact, being a great listener will accelerate your success just as much, perhaps even more, than being a good talker. As all good salespeople will tell you, it's impossible to learn anything from someone else if you are doing all the talking. That's why an anagram of listen is silent. Of course, as a student of failure it's really important you don't use your ears more than you do your mouth. (Some clever git once said we have one mouth and two ears and they should be used in that proportion.) And if you do accidentally slip into the habit of keeping it zipped, for once in a while, make sure you at least continue to listen with prejudice – or in other words pre-judgement. That's what most people do, or as Stephen Covey says: 'Most people do not listen with the intent to understand: they listen with the intent to reply.' Now what did I just say?

[3] OK, maybe not politicians.

create, to speak in front of an audience. And they get plenty of chances because everyone else is running at speed in the opposite direction. So, can you see why, if you are to remain a failure, you must never stop believing that you have all the communication skills of the Hunchback of Notre-Dame on a bad day with his mouth full of golf balls?

Step forty-two

Don't understand the secrets of great teams and great customer service.

Quote to avoid

Those are my principles. If you don't like them I have others. **Groucho Marx**

What's the difference between a team of losers and a team of winners?

What do the winners have that losers don't?

Why am I asking you all these questions?

What if the Hokey Cokey really is what it's all about?

Asda, part say of the Wal-Mart family as they would put it, are one of my favourite clients. Many years ago I did a speaking engagement for them at Asda House, their HQ here in Leeds. Now have you ever had that thing where you visit somewhere for the first time and there is a buzz in the building? (And I'm not talking about faulty fluorescent lights.) There's just something about the place and the people that make it feel special. Well, every time I visit Asda it's always like that. So after that very first visit I thought I want to work with them, but I wasn't exactly sure why apart from being able to say I liked the place, the people and the buzz. Well, from making the decision that I wanted to work with them it took nearly three years before I got any business (see step thirty-seven for the secret of how I kept going).

Eventually I find myself in a top level meeting with the chief executive who I'd only talked to briefly a couple of times before.

So you can imagine that from my point of view there was a lot at stake. Being a good salesman I'm practising the number one skill which, if you read the second footnote on the previous step, you'll know is to listen – or as Stephen Covey would say, I was attempting to 'first understand before being understood'. Finally the moment arrives for me to speak and my opening question is, 'Well thanks for that background to get us started I was wondering which staff do you think will need training first?' at which point the CEO takes a deep breath, puts his hand up and says, 'Steve, before this relationship goes any further can I just point out we don't have any staff.' At this point I thought, 'Well who am I going to bloody train then?' He went on to say, 'No, here we only have colleagues,' to which I remember thinking, 'Oh no it's the Wal-Mart American effect.' Turns out it wasn't that at all. It was explained to me that the cornerstone on how Asda did business was their values. The difference being they didn't just say it but behaved that way.[1] 'Respect for the Individual' was at the heart of how anyone who worked for Asda could expect to be treated. They felt 'staff' immediately says 'us' and 'them', whereas 'colleagues' is just one way of expressing that, whether you stack the shelves or run the company, you are respected.

[1] I once had my car at the garage for a service and I told them that ideally I'd like it back for 4.00 pm. They said that would be fine and would call me when it was ready. Needless to say they never called, so I ended up having to call them. They said the car was ready and I could pick it up right away. I got a lift and told my ride they needn't hang about as my car was ready. I marched up to the service desk and said, 'I'm here for my car,' to which the reply was, 'It's not ready yet.' 'But you said it was.' 'Sorry it'll just be five minutes, why not enjoy a coffee?' So I go over to the coffee area (and by the way, why does the coffee have to be so terrible?) and there hanging on the wall in a gold frame, because it's always in a gold frame, is the dealership's customer pledge. It's the usual guff about how they are prepared to crawl over broken glass for their customers. Now remember, I'm being forced to read this whilst experiencing awful customer care. Worst still, it was 40 minutes before I got my car. So if you really want to annoy people put your values on public display then utterly fail to live up to them. Sweet. We also once did some work with a large financial institution who had a core value of 'Open, honest communication'. Everyone we dealt with acted that way apart from the CEO who told nobody anything. Nice. The message this clearly sends out to both internal and external customers is that we are not serious about this.

There are loads of other ways Asda create a culture of respect, like for example referring to everyone by their first name regardless of their position in the company.

Cut to the second meeting with Asda and the top people person – not being into hierarchies they're not big on titles either – says, 'Eh Steve, have you read this book – we're big fans of it?' Now as the consultant[2] I'm thinking, shouldn't I be telling them which books to read? The book is called *From Good To Great* by Jim Collins. Now if you can't be bothered to read it, which I'm sure is the case, let me sum it up for you. Based on a 15-year research project, the book concludes that if you want to take your organization from good to great, first and foremost you must focus on who is on the bus before you get too hung up on where the bus is going. What does that mean? Well, we've already touched upon the importance of vision, having a clear destination and a plan to get there. But destinations can change and so can the route. However, if you have the right folk on the bus, and they're in the right seats (or in other words they share the same values and behaviours) it won't matter. The secret of great companies, teams and relationships is that they are based on shared values. Just as importantly those values are non-negotiable. In other words, if you are a manager at Asda, you can't respect your people in the morning but then not in the afternoon. Also people who can't live the values will be asked to get off the bus. It's unlikely this will happen very often anyway as the recruitment process is based around the values too.

You may be thinking this is all fluffy pink bunnies,[3] but Asda, and other value driven companies, will tell you it also has a profound effect on the bottom line. Firstly, because people prefer

---

[2] My favourite definition of a consultant is that it is a man who knows one hundred and fourteen different ways to make love BUT doesn't know any women.

[3] Fluffy pink bunnies. I use this expression a lot but have no idea what it means. Why don't you decide for yourself.

THE SECRET of great companies, teams and relationships is that they are based on shared values.

working in an environment where they are treated with respect, you'll find retention rates and performance much higher. (Incidentally, the only way to make it into the annual *Sunday Times* top 100 UK companies to work for is to prove you are living and breathing the values and vision, and that your people can articulate what they are.) Secondly, customers like it too because what they want is consistency of behaviour from whichever bit of the organization they touch. The idea being whether you walk into an Asda in Leeds or in London people act the same. It empowers folk to make brilliant decisions on behalf of customers because they are guided by their values.

However, in the spirit of fairness Asda aren't the only supermarket that have impressed me. Take a look at this letter:

Dear Sir/Madam,

I am writing regarding an incident concerning your store which happened on the evening of Saturday 13th October.

I had sent my idiot husband shopping for some fresh chives, crucial to a recipe I had planned for a dinner party, and he returned with a pot of parsley which had been incorrectly labelled as chives.

Feeling quite cross, I telephoned the store and explained what had happened. I was pleasantly surprised when it was immediately agreed that someone would pop over to my house with some chives.

Unfortunately, when a very nice lady arrived at my house with the chives, they were the wrong kind. The recipe required fresh chives and these were dried. I must have looked very disappointed and the young lady was very concerned but I thanked her anyway and told her not to worry, I'd manage with what I had.

I was shocked, to say the least, when she reappeared some time later, with a pot of fresh chives. She had been so concerned about my dinner party that although Sainsbury's had sold out of fresh chives, she had driven to, shall we say, a rival supermarket! Although it may sound trivial, the fresh herbs really made a difference.

Unfortunately, I didn't get the woman's name, but I'm hoping you will be able to track down this wonderful member of staff and give her all the praise she deserves for her innovation and thoughtfulness. What an asset to the store.

Many thanks and best wishes

Yours sincerely,

Mrs Candy McDermott[4]

Yes I was the idiot husband who doesn't know his chives from his elbow. Thing is, how do you get staff, whoops colleagues, to behave in the exceptional manner of the lady above? In the book *The Nordstrom Way*, author Robert Spector reveals one of the ways Nordstrom create an incredible customer experience: 'Nordstrom's employee handbook is just a five-by-eight-inch grey card that reads: We're glad to have you with our company. Our

---

[4] They did make a fundamental mistake in that they never wrote back. It was only a few weeks later that my wife bumped into the same lady in the supermarket and asked whether the manager had thanked her on our behalf. He had, which was great, but they just hadn't told us.

* This step of the guide holds the record for the number of footnotes. Of course, you will only know this if you have read all the other footnotes. And nobody in their right mind would do that. Skim, skim, skim – that's the way to get through a book. Don't want to go in too deep. You might never get out. Don't want to fill up your brain with too much new stuff otherwise you'll have to empty out some of the old garbage. Of course, you might be one of those detail nuts. You might be tempted to go back through the whole thing counting all the footnotes, but surely you've got other more productive things you could be doing? Like thinking, why don't you ever get gruntled employees or guilty bystanders? What happens if you get scared half to death twice? If something goes without saying why do people say it? I know you can be overwhelmed and underwhelmed but can you just be whelmed? Is there anything easier done than said? Are you still reading this…? Turn the page now…I said turn the page…look you can't keep reading because the footnote stops here. OK…here.

number one goal is to provide outstanding customer service. Set both your personal and professional goals high. We have great confidence in your ability to achieve them: Rule 1: Use your good judgment in all situations. There will be no additional rules. Please feel free to ask your department manager, store manager, or division general manager any question at any time.'

I love that because I can remember it. I know some companies that would need a wheelbarrow to cart their company corporate tosh around in. Hear their monotone chant: 'Here are our eight customer values, ten colleague behaviours and six leadership traits that all our managers must know by heart and follow at all times.' Yeah right.

Action not to take

David Brent from *The Office*, one of the world's leading experts on team building, points out: 'It's the team that matters. Where would The Beatles be without Ringo? If John got Yoko to play drums the history of music would be completely different.'

The secret of great teams is that they have shared values and vision. They are on the bus, they are in the right seat and they know where it's going. The first thing we did when we set up our company The Confident Club was to sit down and decide what our values were going to be. For instance, one of our values can be best expressed as: 'We don't want to work with or for anyone that we wouldn't want to go for a drink with.' We don't believe just because someone can do the job that's enough, or because someone is a paying customer that's enough either. No, if we are going to be spending time with these people we want to like them too. So that's how we decide who we are going to work with. And just as importantly who we aren't going to work with. Our team is made up of different people, with different personalities, with different skills, and different experience, who complement each other. The real secret is because first and foremost we like each other, we get on.

You, however, should try to get by with a team that hate each others' guts and be prepared to tolerate behaviour that goes against everything you hold important and dear. You must never slam on the air brakes at the bus stop and sling the troublemakers off. Once again David Brent summed it up profoundly when he said: 'There's no "I" in team. But then there's no "I" in "useless smug colleague", either. And there's four in "platitude-quoting idiot". Go figure.'

Step forty-three
Don't develop winners and winning relationships.

Quote to avoid

Before you criticize someone, you should walk a mile in their shoes. That way, when you criticize them, you're a mile away and you have their shoes.

Jack Handey

Skinner's[1] behaviour modification principle states: 'Every behaviour you reward you reinforce.' And it doesn't matter whether the behaviour is good or bad. Let's say you are out supermarket shopping with a small child in tow. Being a small child, after not very long, it gets bored but can't get your attention so decides the best course of action will be to hurl itself from its seat in the shopping trolley on to the floor and roll around in a red-faced tantrum screaming, 'Sweets, sweets, sweets,' at the top of its lungs. (Is it possible to scream from the bottom of your lungs?) Now, if your reaction is to scream back, 'Stop embarrassing me,' at the top of your voice (in front of a load of strangers who you will with all probability never see again – but that's beside the point), then according to Skinner what you are doing by giving the child your attention is actually ensuring this kind of behaviour will continue. Much better to catch the child doing something right and tell it, 'It's really good how you are sitting there quietly while I do the shopping.' Clearly Skinner didn't have kids.

[1] The McDermott self-importance principle states: 'Behavioural psychologists will always name principles after themselves.'

The fact is I've found this principle works just as well for big people. If you want to develop winners catch them doing stuff right and praise them. Make sure the praise isn't just flannel or flattery but specific and to the point. Not, 'I really like you,' but, 'One thing I really like about you is...' If you can do it in 60 seconds or less so much the better, because that will make it more memorable and effective. It's also been proven that the best kind of feedback is timely, so tell them as soon as you can about a behaviour you like. Don't save it up for the annual appraisals.

I'm all for praise but not for appraisals. The best management tool ever invented if your goal is to demotivate an entire workforce is the annual appraisal. Don't you love that term 'appraisal'? What a management conceit. To me it says, 'We clever people who run the company with our big superior brains, compared to you lowly workers, if we can find the time may deem to give you the benefit of our profound wisdom by appraising you.' Never of course must they, the workers, be put in a position where they can 'appraise' us back. Well to start with they wouldn't have the skills for it, it's very hard to do, and of course to be a failure in management it's really important you never ask your team what they think of your performance.

THE BEST management tool ever invented if your goal is to demotivate an entire workforce is the annual appraisal.

The reason annual appraisals don't work, if you are attempting to develop winners, is that all we remember is the massive cock-up the person made the week before the appraisal, not all the brilliant things they've been doing the rest of the year. Plus, you spend all the time looking back and 'appraising' past perform-ance rather than spending most of the time looking forward at the exciting year ahead.

When I was a creative director working in an advertising agency, I realized the annual appraisals I was meant to conduct for every member of my department were a waste of time. No matter which side of the fence you were on it was a time of year every-one dreaded. In fact I simply didn't have the time to try and see the whole department in the space of two weeks, which meant quite often individuals' 'appraisals' were put back or cancelled entirely. Of course, the message this sent to them was that they weren't important, again proving 'appraisals' are a lousy way of motivating people.

So I changed. Instead of annual 'appraisals' I switched to regular 'development discussions'. As the term implies these were held on a regular and rolling basis. The rule of thumb being the newer the person, or the newer to the job they were, the more often I would see them for a chat, which in some cases might be once a week. I didn't see everyone at the same time of the year, but they would all have an annual 'development discussion' held on their anniversary of joining the company. This meant, because we had been meeting throughout the year, only 20% of the discussion was about that year and 80% was about their development for the next 12 months. This proved far more motivational for both sides.

One challenge is that so often it's the poor performers who get all the attention because their mistakes stand out like a sore thumb. And you spend all your time telling people off and correcting per-formance. Whereas the best performers have got their heads down and are getting on with it, so that if you're not careful they become invisible to you.

By the way, it's very hard to reprimand someone if you're not already in their good books. If all you do is catch them doing stuff wrong, once you're out of the way, they'll just say to their mates or brothers and sisters, 'All he ever does is tell me off.' Whereas if you praise them much more often than you bollock them they won't be able to do that. Stephen Covey puts it more politely when he says: 'You need to be in the black in their emotional bank account.'

Dale Carnegie said we shouldn't criticize, condemn or complain. When Abraham Lincoln had cause to be mad at one of his generals during the American Civil War he made a point of sitting down and writing them a long letter. He would bluntly spell out exactly what he thought of them, listing all their failings and inadequacies in great detail. He would fill the letter with cynicism, scorn and anger. When he could think of nothing else to write he would take the letter, tear it up and throw it away. Maybe he was just following Benjamin Franklin's advice: 'Remember not only to say the right thing in the right place, but far more difficult, to leave unsaid the wrong thing at the tempting moment.'

I have a rule that I won't indulge in gossip or talk about someone behind their back. I'd rather tell them to their face or not at all. You of course should continue to talk and gossip behind people's backs. Of course, they would never do the same to you.

Action not to take

Don't stop giving all your attention to the people who make the most mistakes or shout the loudest, and continue to ignore those who quietly and efficiently get on with it.

Don't have regular 'development discussions' with your team, and even your kids, but do continue with the wonderful world of 'annual appraisals'. Two questions you wouldn't want to ask are, 'What can you do this year that you couldn't do last year?' (I always wanted to know that my people were growing and learning – I didn't mind if it was something not even to do with work like passing their driving test) and, 'Have you fallen off your bike this year – and if not, why not?' (I felt it important to give people permission to make mistakes just so long as they learnt from them).

Don't catch three people this week doing something right and tell them. (Don't write in your diary, 'Catch three people doing something right,' so you don't forget to do it.)

Actually there is another secret and that's to make sure your praise always outweighs your criticism. If like me you have teenagers here's a Zen saying just for you: 'The surest way to knock the chip off someone's shoulder is by patting them on the back.' So don't do that either.

Step forty-four

Don't step up. Don't do extraordinary things.

Quote to avoid

'The difference between what we do and what we are capable of doing would suffice to solve most of the world's problems.' **Gandhi**

So as we near the end of this guide you now know what it takes to be a failure. But here is one almost final thought for you to contemplate. Are life's success stories about extraordinary people doing extraordinary things or are they about ordinary people doing extraordinary things? Are they about extraordinary businesses doing extraordinary things or plain, ordinary businesses doing extraordinary things?

Here is how someone extremely bright once summed it up: 'In my view, wherever you find success, you will find some ordinary person, like you or I, who decided to raise the bar. An individual or an organization who said: "We are going to be the best we can be." The key is they chose something that they really, I mean really, wanted to do, come hell or high water. We may think of people like Olympic athletes as the only ones who come from this mould, but that's not the case. Olympians may only train for four years, the people I'm talking about often train for a lifetime to reach their goals. They have even more discipline than some of the greatest sports stars. More commitment than all but a few. A bigger dream than most. A sense of purpose that all but consumes them. A passion, fire, energy and enthusiasm pervades everything they do. At the start, there are many things they can't

OLYMPIANS may only
train for four years,
the people I'm talking about
often train for a
lifetime
to reach their goals.

do, but they are prepared to learn. To do whatever it takes. Yet they seek out the maximum amount of fun and enjoyment as they travel the road towards realizing their dreams. That's very easy because they don't ever feel like they're striving for something, only ever stretching. So stress is something they don't suffer from much. Besides, they believe in the old saying, "It's better to travel than arrive." However, they are very careful who they choose as their travelling companions. You may think these people are rare, special or somehow gifted. Or just plain lucky. I know different. Look around you. Put away your excuses. Open your eyes a little wider and you'll see these are plain, ordinary people. They just decided they deserved to lead extraordinary lives.'

I don't know if you know who said that. Actually, it was me. Not a bad summary of all the feel-good claptrap you mustn't listen to if you wish to fail. What I didn't quite manage to cram into the above would be a final thought on the choice between apathy or action (to be honest, I couldn't really be bothered). Apathy or action? One of these will get you everything you deserve. What is it you deserve again?

Action not to take

Don't have a goal to be in the top 10% of people, or organizations, who do what you do. That alone will cause you to do extraordinary things. Don't realize, even as you read this, that this is the last chance before a few more weeks, months or years flash by for you to get your finger out and do something about your sad excuse for a life, career or business. Don't think that David Thoreau knew what he was talking about when he said: 'I learned this: that if you advance confidently in the direction of your dreams and endeavour to live the life which you have imagined, you will meet with a success unexpected in common hours.'

Step forty-four-and-a-half

Don't stop doing everything by halves, that's if you do anything at all.

Quote to avoid

'Enthusiasm is one of the most powerful engines of success. When you do a thing, do it with your might. Put your whole soul into it. Stamp it with your own personality. Be active, be energetic, be enthusiastic and faithful, and you will accomplish your objective. Nothing great was ever achieved without enthusiasm.' **Ralph Waldo Emerson**

When Julius Caesar invaded Britain he decided to have a quick question and answer session with his massed ranks of legionnaires on the cliff tops, above what is now Dover, before they went in search of their first battle with the ancient Britons. 'So, who has the first question?' said Caesar. One of the soldiers' hands went up. 'Great Caesar, is it true that these Britons have thousands of fierce war machines, with sharp blades that stick out from the wheels, designed to cut our men's legs off at the knees?' 'Umm . . .' murmured Caesar. 'I don't know the answer to that one, but are there any more questions?' A second soldier's hand shot up. 'Oh mighty Caesar, is it true these Britons are ten feet tall, have two heads and cover their naked bodies in blue paint to scare the enemy before they go into battle?' 'Don't know that either,' replied Caesar with a hunch of his shoulders. 'Right lads, I've just got time for one more question before we get stuck in,' shouted Caesar. A timid hand went up from the ranks. 'Caesar, I've heard these Britons are led by a fierce warrior queen

STAY AWAY
FROM THESE

and have sworn to her they will die to the last man rather than surrender,' said a worried looking Centurion. 'Sorry lads, I don't know the answer to that either,' responded Caesar. 'But what I do know,' he continued, 'is that if you look down on the beach, I've burnt all the boats, so we'd better win!'

Emerson says that enthusiasm is one of the most powerful engines of success. And he is dead right. But more important than enthusiasm, to your ultimate success or failure, will be your level of commitment. Several years ago when I left a well-paid job to go off into the world of the self-employed, the common response from many of my former colleagues was, 'Well, if it doesn't work out you can always come back.' Thing is, I'd burnt my boats, so I couldn't. The other thing most people said was, 'I couldn't handle the insecurity of being self-employed. Not knowing where my next pay cheque was coming from.' At first I believed them, until I realized I had more security than them. No

MORE IMPORANT than

enthusiasm, to your

ultimate success

or failure, will be your level

of commitment.

one could fire me, but me. And unlike their fixed salary, there was no limit to what I could earn. Sure, people thought I should be committed, and I was. Trouble is they meant to a secure unit for the insane.

Now remember the quote from our brainy friend Goethe in step six? Of course you don't. I mean the one where he was talking about increasing the number of unforeseen incidents and meetings and material assistance that we enjoy in life by increasing our level of commitment. 'Until one is committed, there is always hesitancy, the chance to draw back . . .' Well, he also said: 'Whatever you can do, or dream you can, begin it. Boldness has genius, magic and power in it. Begin it now.' This one quote had a profound impact on a guy who came on one of my boat workshops. His name is David Taylor and he is the production director for a highly successful design company and now lives in the beautiful city of Sydney, Australia. But that wasn't always the case. Here's how David tells it.

'Steve, when I came on your boat workshop you covered a lot of things, but the one thing that did it for me was that quote from that German bloke. Now I'm from Yorkshire (remember we are blunt speakers) and I would translate what he was saying to mean, "Dave, nobody is going to do it for you, you need to get off your arse, stop making excuses and do it for yourself." Let me tell you about my circumstances back then. We were living in an ex-council house in Huddersfield that we'd bought off the council because it seemed a good idea at the time. Naturally, it being our first house, we were proud and spent lots of time and money making it as nice as possible. Then, for some unknown reason, things started to go wrong. The estate, and the behaviour of the people living on the estate, took a real turn for the worse. People started dumping their rubbish in our garden, threatening our kids on the way to school, the crime rate soared and lots of the houses around about us became boarded up and derelict. Me and my wife thought, that's it, we are stuck here for ever. I mean, who in their right mind would now want to buy our house?

'Then I listened to what Goethe had to say on your workshop and began to think. It was June at the time, and that night when I got home, I immediately said to my wife, "Good news we are moving out on the 3rd of January." She said, "But where to and how?" I said, "I don't know, but what I do know is we are moving out on the 3rd of January." You see, I had also learned that if you have a really big why, and a when, then you will do whatever it takes to find the how. She thought I was crazy. Even so, I put our house up for sale. But do you know what, as soon as I made that decision, things changed. I now believed we could do it and started to notice things that had simply passed me by before. Like the tiny advertisement for bridging loans from a small building society. I took out a loan and we bought a nice house in a great area. We still hadn't sold our house and my wife was frantic, but I just kept saying, "We are moving out on the 3rd of January and if I have to I'll board the house up until we sell it." Obviously with the bridging loan I only had a few weeks' grace before it would be financially impossible to pay for both houses, but I was now committed to finding a solution.

'Anyway, come January 3rd there is the removal van outside our house, we're moving but the house still isn't sold. I'm stood by the back of the van when who should walk past but the head-mistress from our children's school. She stops and says, "Hello Mr Taylor, I knew you were moving because your children have left to go to their new school, it's just I never knew you lived here. Do you know, I think this is the best, most beautifully looked after house on the estate. I've been thinking about moving nearer to the school, I'm sick of all the travelling I have to do. I know it's not the best of areas but I don't mind that for the extra conven-ience. I know it's a bit late to ask, but by any chance is the house still for sale?"'

What do you think David said? Now there are two ways of looking at this. Either David made it happen or he is the luckiest man on the planet. I'll leave you to decide.

You may have heard of the actress Lana Turner. The story goes she was working as a waitress in a Hollywood coffee shop when she was discovered by a movie producer. Is the equivalent of that going to happen to you? No. I'm not even sure it really happened to her. It is more likely an invented PR story that appeals to our nature of wanting something for nothing and firmly believing in luck. To remain a failure, don't stop waiting to be discovered. Don't stop waiting for a producer to show up. Don't go produce yourself instead. You see, if you continue to wait, you won't practise being the best you can be, which means even when an opportunity does arise, you won't be ready.

TO REMAIN a failure,
don't stop waiting to be discovered.

Action not to take

Here is absolutely the last thing not to do. Don't burn your boats. Don't take Norman Vincent Peale's advice, who says: 'Throw your heart over the fence and the rest will follow.' Instead be half-hearted in all your endeavours. Don't ensure that when the going gets tough, and it will, there is no going back. Don't create a level of commitment that means the only way of going is forward. Don't stop believing in the myth of security. Or that some knight in shining armour will one day turn up to save you.

And a final thought, before you put down this guide and use it to prop open a door, if you try to fail and you succeed, what have you done?

Disclaimers

Disclaimer to step seven

Remember the bit at the very front of the book – I know it's ages ago – about 'thinking styles' and how the test of first-rate intelligence is the ability to hold two opposing ideas in your mind at the same time. Well let's test that now. SMARTS goals are rubbish and don't work. Actually I'm being a bit extreme with that statement but I just wanted to wake you up. What I've found is that for some people SMARTS are the absolute, ideal way to go about setting their goals. The process appeals to the logical part of their brain. However for others, SMARTS are a real turn off. They don't like them because they don't engage them on an emotional level. More importantly they don't produce the promised results. There are alternatives that fulfil the same role as SMARTS but will appeal to those who prefer to use the more imaginative part of their brain. Here the idea is to create a dominant thought pattern, or if you like a sensory rendering of the goal. To see, feel and hear yourself as you achieve it. Michael Heppell, in his excellent book *How to be Brilliant*, calls this the three Ps. He says when you set goals, first of all they need to be Personal; second, they need to be Positive; and third, they must be Present tense. Personal means the goal is for you, Positive is you think about what you want rather than what you don't want and Present tense is thinking about the goal as if you've already achieved it.

The point I'm making is successful people experiment until they find a goal setting system that suits them and their personality. But they don't leave it to chance by having no system at all. Some people will swear by SMARTS and writing everything down in great detail. Others would prefer to put their goals in pictures, sounds and feelings (even smells and tastes), and create a dominant thought pattern. Some will do both because they want to engage the power of both the left and right parts of their brain.

Here's a final way to improve results from goal setting. Remember Phil in step seven, well like lots of people I know, he doesn't settle for just having Achievable and Realistic goals. He also has some that are Awesome and Ridiculous. That's because when he stops and thinks of anyone he admires, one of his heroes, he knows they didn't think in terms of what was realistic or achievable (people like Mother Teresa, Madonna, Muhammad Ali, Mozart). He totally agrees with Helen Keller, who said: 'One can never consent to creep when one feels an impulse to soar.'

Plus, when you reach a realistic, achievable goal, it's not that exciting; it's usually something well within your current capability, based on what you've done so far. Whereas awesome, ridiculous, is based on the idea that the past doesn't equal the future. What you've done up until now isn't important, it's what you are going to do from now. These kinds of goals stretch you. Do you always get to this level? No. But Phil has found that half an awesome, ridiculous goal is usually on average twice an achievable, realistic one. And he'd rather have that. This is just one more reason why you don't want to think big. You certainly don't want to do what Ted Turner, one of the most successful media moguls on the planet, suggests, which is to set goals you can't achieve in your own lifetime.

Disclaimer to step seventeen

For those of you foolish enough to be pondering doing the exact opposite of the steps suggested in this guide, be careful with this step. We know that fantastically successful individuals don't always bother with a parachute. They figure the more the risk, the bigger the step, the more there is to learn, the more there is to gain. Whatever happens they don't let it affect their self-esteem. This must be why, on average, millionaires lose their fortune three times before they learn how to keep it for good. (I guess once you've made a million, making another million from scratch doesn't seem that hard. It's an attitude summed up in the saying, 'You can't leap a chasm in two strides,' whatever the hell that means.)

Answers

Answer to the longest word in this guide: electroencephalographic (step twenty-nine).

Answer to the most obscure reference: Northern Soul (steps twenty-seven and thirty). An underground music scene that flourished in the north of England, particularly at Blackpool Mecca and Wigan Casino, between the early and late 1970s when I was just a lad. For the incredibly tiny percentage of Northern Soul fans reading this, 'Keep the faith'. And did you ever visit the Variety Club (sometimes known as The Okey Club) in Keighley on a Sunday night? Top spot.